The Mind of Christ

"Yesterday, Today and Forever"

JOYce Mary Brenton

BALBOA.
PRESS
A DIVISION OF HAY HOUSE

Balboa Press books may be ordered through booksellers or by contacting:

Balboa Press
A Division of Hay House
1663 Liberty Drive
Bloomington, IN 47403
www.balboapress.com
1 (877) 407-4847

Because of the dynamic nature of the Internet, any web addresses or links contained in this book may have changed since publication and may no longer be valid. The views expressed in this work are solely those of the author and do not necessarily reflect the views of the publisher, and the publisher hereby disclaims any responsibility for them.

The author of this book does not dispense medical advice or prescribe the use of any technique as a form of treatment for physical, emotional, or medical problems without the advice of a physician, either directly or indirectly. The intent of the author is only to offer information of a general nature to help you in your quest for emotional and spiritual well-being. In the event you use any of the information in this book for yourself, which is your constitutional right, the author and the publisher assume no responsibility for your actions.

Any people depicted in stock imagery provided by Thinkstock are models, and such images are being used for illustrative purposes only. Certain stock imagery © Thinkstock.

Print information available on the last page.

ISBN: 978-1-5043-3043-5 (sc)
ISBN: 978-1-5043-3045-9 (hc)
ISBN: 978-1-5043-3044-2 (e)

Library of Congress Control Number: 2015904695

Balboa Press rev. date: 5/21/2015

Dedication

We dedicate these humble messages to all our brothers
and sisters who daily seek the Mind of Christ with
all their hearts, minds, souls and strength.

RECEIVER'S STATEMENT

It all began almost 40 years ago with one scripture.... "Seek ye first the kingdom of heaven and *all* these things shall be added unto you."

At that time, I was living my life a little above the poverty level and in a very unhappy marriage. I was searching for some kind of God-given help and the answer seemed simple. Please understand that it wasn't really any overdose of spirituality I was seeking. I wanted the material blessings I thought the above scripture represented.

In my materialistic mind I took that particular scripture to mean I should simply get up early and the first thing every morning I was to seek the things of the Kingdom. And at that time I believed heavy duty Kingdom living meant scripture study and prayer. I began a daily practice of journaling my prayers and I have never missed.

Shortly after I awoke each morning, in a large wire-bound notebook, I began this ongoing journaling process. For the most part most of those early journal entries were major venting experiences mixed liberally with prayers of supplication for release from my less than happy circumstances. I found no difficulty venting and easily filled quite a few pages daily.

Occasionally I would take a breather, and in those infrequent breaks the Still Small Voice began to insert a few words... then a few one-liners that I recognized as powerful... definitely getting my attention.

Why? Amazing wisdom! Way, way, way beyond my limited realm of rationality! I was receiving very sound advice, telling me to do things I would never tell myself to do. I knew I wasn't talking to my self.

Over the years the practice developed into my simply listening, with no more venting or supplication. I was simply taking dictation. And this continues to this very day.

During those early days of our budding friendship, Jesus once said that He could speak to me 24/7 but my attention span was far too limited.

I have filled years and years of lap-size wire-bound notebooks with these wonderful messages. And I have thrown them all away, believing that if the tablets were ever discovered by my family after my death they would think me quite insane.

The only reason these messages became public at all is because I got involved with a spiritual group where I was encouraged to ask Jesus if He would give some messages on a regular basis for the group. I asked, and the very next day the messages for ears other than mine came forth.

That's about it. It would please me if the reader would understand that anyone may receive messages from the heavenly realm. It doesn't take any special talent or gift, or any measure of holiness. I could tell some gruesome stories of my personal life that would rationally discount God actually talking to a person like me, and yet in all these years of our friendship, I *never* heard one word of condemnation.

Anyone can journal with God. I believe that with my whole heart and soul. On a personal level though, I had to get a bit of my venting out of the way first before I could learn to listen. God was very patient with me and is *very* patient with all of us.

JOYce Mary Brenton
January 2014

Just imagine it is the day before Christmas and you are invited to a little intimate dinner party on Christmas day where Jesus, our Teacher, will be present as one of our invited Guests. Can you imagine what His Words to us might be on the day of His Birthday Celebration?

CHRISTMAS MESSAGE

"And the Word became flesh and dwells among us."

"This is the day you choose to celebrate My birth. I AM here with you now. And that will *never* change. You and I walk in Our Father's Will each day, to extend His unconditional love to all we meet upon the Path. To live with Me is to live and move and breathe as an expression of His Love to all our Brothers and Sisters.

Today is a day to celebrate Love. Give the gift of Love as freely as you have received it. Simply love one another as I love you.

Father has given these instructions throughout the centuries through every true prophet of His Will. There will never be a variance to this Gospel of Truth. And My Message to you will never vary, My Brothers and Sisters. The true message has always been the same.

It is a beautiful day, this day of birthday celebration. This is the holiday of Love, but Love is to be lived *all* the days of our lives. Can you extend the rules of love into tomorrow and all the days that follow? Of course you can! Love is all we are. And that, too, will never change."

See your self... Seated at this birthday celebration, perhaps seated to the right or left of this One of great renown. He asks you if you (personally) can extend the Father's Love into all your tomorrows? He tells you, beloved child of God, that "you can." Will you try? Begin today!

Now suppose you have come to the last day of the year and the New Year waits for you just around the corner of today. Can you imagine what Jesus, Our Teacher, our older, wiser Brother might express to us as we welcome the new birth of our New Year?

New Year's Eve Message

It has been an interesting year, has it not, My Brothers and Sisters? Of course! There have been many days of mysteries solved. You and I have come far on the Path, but in truth we have far to go and much to accomplish in the year ahead.

There can be a little apprehension as we turn the corner from the old year into the new but take heart, for I *will* take your hand each day. Our friendship grows ever stronger. We have an unbreakable bond between us that will allow the tasks to become easier.

Yes, today has its challenges, but all the lessons of the days are for your growth. We have planned this day well. Walk it in joy! In joy for the progress you have made and in joy for the great progress in the days ahead.

Your trust is high. Let us proceed with *all* apprehension behind us.

> *See your self*…right now in this very moment…going into the New Year with Jesus holding your hand in His, each and every day, in an "unbreakable bond" allowing all your tasks to become easier. How wonder-filled a thought is that? Ah, indeed, most wonderful!

And just suppose, precious child of God, you could actually meet with Him each and every day, sitting attentively at His Feet, as it were. Would He have messages to give you? Messages to help you personally along the Path? Is this possible?

Yes, each day a new beginning for you, hand in hand with Him, for such a time as this.

JANUARY

January 1
For Your Continual Growth

"I welcome you now to this New Year, My beloved Brothers and Sisters.

Do you remember when, as children, you returned to school after summer vacation? You wondered about the new teacher you would have, and whether you could handle the new curriculum? You were apprehensive.

The New Year lies ahead in much the same way now as it was then. You will have many lessons to learn. And the curriculum of life is ever changing; of that you can be very sure. But we go together, you and I. You do not walk alone.

The Path is programmed *always* for your continual growth."

> *See your self...* Walking hand in hand with the Creator of this Universe, facing fearlessly *all* that lies ahead. And the Path *is* programmed, designed as it were, exactly for you and your continual growth.

January 2
Fill The Pockets Of Your Hearts

"Step by step the Kingdom is advanced, and lesson by lesson the Ambassadors of His Will advance also.

1

You are not the same person who ventured forward through last year and now into this one, and you will hardly recognize yourselves with the advancements of this New Year.

You *will* advance mightily in His Principles of Love. But do not hurry. The Kingdom advances one step at a time, one lesson at a time. Simply follow the rules each day.

Arise each morning and do a little weeding in the gardens of your thinking. Then simply fill the pockets of your hearts with the seeds of love and venture forward to do the Will of our Father."

See your self... ah, stretching the imagination a bit, see your heart with pockets to be filled with seeds of love, and yes, go about spreading these seeds liberally throughout your day. "But do not hurry." Yes, the Kingdom advances, one step at a time and "lesson by lesson."

January 3
God Is Love Within You

"Our Father is Love incarnate in each and every one of you. You are His Hands to extend His gentle Touch. He uses your lips to smile and give the kind words that He wishes to give to all His Children everywhere.

You are His Ministers of Love and you will serve His Will all the days of your lives. We will persist in His Love until "the Paradise of His Intent" becomes reality. We have a worthy goal and we know exactly where we go.

Onward in Love! The summit is in sight. The reality of His Kingdom is at hand."

See your self... fully equipped by your Creator with hands, and feet, lips and tongue as ministers to His Holy Will. Recognize this very day your value in creating the "paradise of His Intent." Smile often!

January 4
Love One Another

"Today I would speak to you of the command to love one another. For some of you, love seems easy. And to others there is little understanding of love.

To those of you who were reared as children with little love – and the numbers are countless – the concept is difficult. Many of you have gone in and out of the feelings of what you call love with little or no satisfaction.

Let me tell you now with no condemnation, that *few* understand love at all. It is Father's Plan that you learn about Love.

The Plan never varies. But the lessons of the New Year will vary, for we must progress ever forward. Nonetheless, the Divine Plan is the same; "Yesterday, Today and Forever."

> *See your self...* entering this New Year as a willing student, understanding that you do not number in the few who understand love, but accepting the curriculum whatever it may be as all inclusive to the Divine Plan. You *will* learn to Love one another.

January 5
An Adventure In Love

"Good morning, My Children.

You have a concept that has come to you from the scripture, that to love you must obey. Have I instructed that you love one another? Most assuredly I have.

To discover what love truly is - the study - the lesson must remain constant. So let us begin today an adventure in the word love. Let us begin with one little step towards the fulfillment of the command to love one another. And know full well, as you take that step, we take that step *together.*"

See your self... "together" with this Beloved Teacher, stepping into the role of His student on an adventure into the curriculum of love. Ah, and what a most amazing adventure it will be!

January 5
A Good Place To Begin

"Let us begin today with one single idea, a starting place, as it were, in the definition of love. Love is kind. That is a good place to begin.

Are you kind? Can you be kind today? Think about your childhood. Were you kind as little children? Most of you had days of kindness.

Now let us build on that word. It is an easy command to be kind today. Simply be kind to one another. A kind word here and there could be a gift you give to Father, for He is *very* kind to you. If I were to ask you today to be kind to one another, to speak kindly to one another, could you do it? Would you do it?"

See your self... as the obedient student, stepping into this day with the goal of service to kindness. You can give this gift. He wouldn't suggest you doing it, if it were impossible to do.

January 7
Kindness is Love's Insignia

"Kindness is an insignia of love, My beloveds. Be kind to one another. Do all you can to make the Path easier to tread for the brothers and sisters who accompany you.

Is there a kindness you can perform today to help someone? Can you lighten someone's burden by your loving assistance? Even a gentle kind word can do so much to make another's burden less burdensome.

Learn to spread the Love of God abroad."

See your self... a student of kindness. Even a simple smile given to one to whom few smiles are ever given is a great kindness, indeed!

January 8
Our Father Is Pleased

"My beloved brothers and sisters, the Father loves you as no other could ever love you. He forgives your *every* mistake and error. He *fully* understands your inability to fully understand.

Our Father is so pleased as day by day we take forward steps on this pathway to Him, in our journey of Love."

See your self... becoming more aware, arriving at a newer understanding of our Father's great love for each of His children, and yes, also a new awareness of His pleasure over each of our forward steps to Him.

January 9
Love Is The Great Mystery

"My children, My words to you today continue our lessons on love, for is love not a very great mystery and worthy of our attention?

Let us think of the mother's love. There are many variations on that love. While some mothers seem to know exactly what to do, some mothers are fearful of their first newborn child. In learning all the ins and outs of the new relationship with this precious gift, she may falter. Even so, the love between the mother and child grows. A bonding between the two occurs.

Would you say that this love relationship then is a work between the two? Ah, yes, it is a labor of love. And the truth is that love grows.

An eternal bond grows also between the Father and His children, children such as you are."

See your self... eternally bonded in an ongoing love relationship with our Heavenly Father. Everything and everyone grows with love.

January 10
A Labor of Love

"Love is always a *labor* and it *always* grows. So when I tell you to simply be kind to one another, for many of you that is a work, indeed, a labor of love.

For those many of you who have lost the way to love, you must begin with small halting steps.

Simple kindness is a labor in love that provides a great place to start the love adventure.

Today be kind to one another, and if there is one for whom it is difficult to extend even one simple kindness, know full well that the words "Whatsoever you do to the least of these, you do unto Me" are indeed My words, words from the very heart of God our Father."

See your self... deeply focused on this one simple rule for today, a rule from the very heart of our loving Father. Be kind to one another. It's not always easy but you can do it or again I remind you, our Teacher would not even expect you to try.

January 11
An Everyday Experience

"I ask you again to simply be kind to one another. You do not need to take a great leap into love, for that is how many of you have caused yourselves great pain. Let us simply say that with so little understanding of what love is, it is better to take the lessons one day at a time and allow the curriculum to become part of your every day experience."

See your self... slowing down with the curriculum. If the Teacher tells us we will cause ourselves less pain by accepting one day at a time, surely we can recognize the need for focus on *no need to hurry* with *His* lesson Plan.

January 12
Endless Supply

"Our Father is our Eternal Source. Thus we go forth today prepared to share the love of God in endless supply.

Expect to be surprised each day by the generosity of our Father's abundant giving. Open your eyes and see with His Eyes. See all the places for your giving, and be prepared to receive without ceasing from the generosity of His unlimited and truly boundless love.

Would you know more about love? Then come and sit with Me awhile. I *will* show you the way."

See your self... more aware of our Father's *boundless* generosity. Waking up to the reality of Father's Love is definitely a part of the lesson Plan. The Way Shower uses the "will" word to signify your success with the curriculum.

January 13
Smile Often Today

"My Children, another beautiful new day begins and our adventure continues.

There have been some successes now in our kindness journey. And today there *will* be moments again for the choice to be kind rather than unkind.

You are surprised at the ease of all of this. You are surprised that all you needed was a little reminder to be kind.

Smile often today. A smile can be a very great gift to a stranger passing by who might be on a journey with little to smile about.

Let your day be full of kindness and many smiles, for you are truly Ambassadors of the Father's Love. It is a very rich legacy you bear as Children of God. You will find much delight in the simplicity of kindness."

See your self... dispensing smiles often today. It's a gift so easily given and it is the insignia that marks us all as Ambassadors of our Father's heavenly Kingdom on earth.

January 14
The Path Grows Easier

"You do well. You need to appreciate yourself more. You need to see that the steps you take now are all forward steps. You come eagerly now each day for My words. You are beginning to truly trust that I will be here for your lessons each day.

We have quite an exciting adventure ahead in this journey on the Path of Love. Your understanding will grow with each day that passes.

Trust the process. There is no hurry. There is plenty of time. You will find that we are very patient and most delighted with every victory. It becomes easier to walk the Path as we walk together."

See your self... delighted with the idea that the adventure grows easier each day, walking hand in hand with the Creator of the very Path we tread each day. And every lesson is specifically designed for each and every one of His amazing Creations.

January 15
Love Centered On You

"As I have said before, we do not count your *supposed* errors. And as the days progress, you *will* grow less hard on your Self. Yes, this is also a very great adventure in trust. You *will* trust the wisdom of these lessons.

And yes, another beautiful day dawns and yes, it is beautiful because you are taking great forward steps in these lessons in love.

You have My love centered on you. You have *always* had My love. There has never been one moment that there has been separation, nor could there ever be."

> *See your self...* in the most amazing love relationship you
> could ever experience. See *now* this perfect relationship and
> know it's unending, *never* to be duplicated and blossoming
> daily by your very new awareness of its existence. Amazing,
> indeed! Ah, and its very notable that there is no accounting
> of your supposed errors.

January 16
The Doorway To Peace

"Good morning, My children. Are you finding it a little easier to be kind? Has there been a few times now when an unkind word was stopped before it passed your lips? Of course, there are moments when you speak too quickly, when the unkind words are loosed without thinking of the consequences. But this is a new era for you.

You are now beginning the *worthy* process of learning the meaning of unconditional love, for you have certainly been on the receiving end of conditional love for most of your days in this mortal existence. You know how many times you have been hurt; by another brother or sister's unkind words or actions. You feel sometimes that to love unconditionally is impossible. Release that thought.

And I say again, there is no hurry in the study of our beautiful and yes, very worthy curriculum.

Another day of kindness lies ahead. A few simple acts of kindness, is all I ask. And as you take these steps, you will find your Self on the doorstep to peace."

> *See your self...* answering His request. A few little acts of kindness will take you to the doorstep of peace. Could it be that simple? Could you have missed the doorstep by being unkind? Absolutely!

January 17
The Path Of Truth

"Yes, this is a special day and we will continue to clarify the rules for Kingdom Living until you have them indelibly committed to memory; until you know no other path to tread but this Path of Truth.

The path seems sometimes full of rocks that cause your feet to stumble. Know full well, you do not tread this Path alone. We go with you every step of the way. You are moving forward.

Have you not often wondered where the doorway is to that elusive thing called peace? You are about to discover its presence often.

Continue as you are going. We delight in every step you take. We delight to see the rocks and boulders of unlove removed from your Path. You are removing those rocks and boulders yourselves."

> *See your self...* involved in *all* that is necessary to remove *every* unkind act from your personal pathway. Indeed, unkindness is a large rock of stumbling, blocking the doorway to peace.

January 18
No Idle Thought

"I tell you now that if there is *anyone* to whom you cannot freely extend the gift of kindness, then you must examine more closely the command to "forgive one another as your Father in Heaven *has* forgiven you. This is no idle thought from the Mind of God."

See your self... already forgiven (past tense) by your Father in Heaven. It's done! Jesus asks you to do the same. Release any and all the captives you may be holding to the unkindness of your own unforgiving mindset. It's essential to release *all* from the bondage of unforgiveness.

And underline "no idle thought from the Mind of God." There are no idle thoughts from our Heavenly Father. None!

January 19
Something New Is Happening

"Good morning, My children.

You awake today with a new excitement. Something new is happening in your days. You are discovering something new in your life. You can be kind. And some of you can be more kind than you thought possible.

You have extended the grace of kindness to those to whom you thought you could not extend kindness and you were successful. And in so doing, you did pass through the doorway to peace a few times.

Having touched the grace of peace, you have decided that more than a taste is necessary."

See your self... in the ministry of kindness. And the taste of peace every now and then is not quite enough for your peace-starved soul. More kindness equals more peace. It's not always easy to give this gift of kindness but worth the effort.

11

January 20
To All You Meet

"Do not hesitate today to extend the hand of kindness to *all* you meet. For in the extension of your kindness, you delight our Father – of that truth you can be very sure.

And so this day becomes a little easier than the day before. And what of the smiles? You are smiling more, too.

Your life circumstances have not altered much, but you cannot say that you are the same. You have taken a step forward on the Path, and for some of you it has been a leap of faith.

You have discovered something very interesting about your Self. You are kind.

And as you extend your hand to one another in kindness, you will see that it is possible to be the cause, to be a partner as it were, in bringing your Brothers and Sisters higher and higher with you on the climb."

> *See your self...* bringing delight as a gift to our Father as we extend our kindness gifts to others. Oh, such a joyful thought that we might gift the One Who so endlessly gifts us.

January 21
You Who Are Kind Are Love.

"I have said that love is kind. And so, you are love. In such a few days of our adventure you have discovered that you are love.

A simple principle, yes, and we will repeat this principle now, so that we are sure you understand. You are kind, and love is kind; and so you are love.

Yes, this is another day to simply be kind to one another. Our Father is *very* pleased with your progress in kindness. Simply continue as you are."

See your self... giving pleasure to the receiver of your kind acts, as well as giving pleasure to your Self for extending the gift of kindness. Ah, but to see Father as *very* pleased with you and your progress; isn't that the most delightful of thoughts for today?

January 22
Give Through Your Smile

"I have told you to smile often. And you are learning to give freely as you have freely received.

Understand that to give and to receive are one and the same. Step happily now into the *gift* of this beautiful day. You are His most beloved Children in whom He is well pleased."

See your self... smiling often for, indeed, you are His *"most beloved"* child.

January 23
Father's Love Surrounds You

"Yes, a new day begins. It has moments of the known and unknown. Today may hold some places of trouble, but your peace need not be troubled. You may rest assured through every moment of today in the knowledge that you are love. And you are loved in a love unchanged.

The Father's Love goes with you, surrounds you in its perfection. And I will tell you again that *all* is well."

See your self... surrounded completely in *perfect* love never failing. No matter what failures you seem to encounter, Father's Love never changes.

January 24
The Ascending Path

"Good morning, My Children. You are not alone on this journey. We go with you every step of the way, as do all your Brothers and Sisters. Yes, we are all in this together.

You hear the tales of those who do not know how to love one another. There are those who seem to have lost the way. No, they are not lost! You are *all* in this together. It is a stairway, and you are all on different steps, but all climbing – quickly? Some very slowly – but do not fear!

I will say those words to you often. You will hear Me say, No fear! No worry! And yes, no hurry either. And I will also say, do not look to the left or to the right. Be content to know we take your hand and offer daily guidance on the Path. Be content to know that you do climb steadily forward."

See you self… hand in hand with Jesus. Yes, never alone! Fully trusting in that reality *will* remove fearful and worrisome thoughts about this Path we tread together. And He says there is no need to hurry. If only we could hurry far less than we consistently do.

January 25
Little Gift Of Love

"Let us continue today with acts of kindness. And as you come to the end of the beautiful gift of this day, ask yourself if you were kind to one on this earthly Path with you.

Did you offer a smile to one who seemed without even the blessing of a smile to return? And were you surprised to find that even a stranger, one you did not know, was eager to return immediately your little gift of love?

Smile often! Be kind!"

See your self... each day asking the simple question – was I kind today? Did I remember my smile as a gift so easily given? Ah, and so free a gift to extend on this journey we take together to be about our Father's Business.

January 26
Peace And Contentment

"Be content! Ah, a new word perhaps to some of you. What is contentment? It is another word for confidence, and yes, trust. Have great confidence in our guidance. We *will* take you to the highest places.

You will be amazed at the peace and simple contentment you will experience as you take even these beginning baby steps in kindness.

Ah, and indeed, the journey grows easier as you give even these seemingly simplest of the gifts of love."

See you self... content and very relaxed as the lessons unfold. And imagine the days that are coming where contentment never wavers. It is possible. With God all things are possible.

January 27
The Doorway To Peace

"Good morning, My children. Today we will begin the study in peace. I have promised to give you that peace that passes all understanding. And I have said you have very little understanding of love. Therefore, elusive peace has very much to do with your ability to love as the Father wills that you love.

We touched briefly a few days ago on the subject of *elusive* peace. Why do you experience so little peace in your life? Why is the experience you all seek so fleeting?

Sometimes you enter through the doorway, but your stay is so brief; the moment is over so quickly. It is challenging for you to stay in peace, isn't it?

You know now that when you are kind, when you offer kindness, you experience peace. You have experienced peace often now with these simple acts of kindness.

You know that when you are kind to one another, you are completely within the Father's Will to extend love in this manner. To be kind is the Father's Will and you are then in the peace that passes understanding."

> *See your self...* fulfilling the greatest commandment to love one another as the Father in Heaven loves you. Can this commandment be so simple in its fulfillment as being kind and thus loving one another? Yes! And is there a reward for compliance to His Will? Yes, Indeed, the peace that passes all understanding.

January 28
Live Always In Peace

"Now I will say to you, if you understand the simple principle to extend kindness always, to maintain peace, you could live always in peace. And if you could do that, our lessons could end now. It is an easy principle in theory, but not in application.

Kindness brings peace. When you are unkind, you enter into unrest, unlove, and yes, you are at war with the world as well as yourself.

I would ask you again today to be kind to *everyone*. And I would say to continue as you are, in peace, for it is My desire that you experience the peace that passes understanding throughout your entire life."

> *See your self...* extending kindness to everyone as the fulfillment of *His desire* for our continual peace. Every war ever fought with all the maiming cruelty had as its basis, the inability of its perpetrators to be kind to one another.

January 29
In And Out Of The Doorway

"Continued discipline *will* reap a great reward. And there is *no greater reward* than peace.

I do not desire that you go in and out of the doorway of peace. Fleeting visits in and out of the Kingdom of Heaven is not the Father's Will for His children.

Come in and stay in, at least long enough to take to heart the lessons each day. You *will* learn to appreciate these lessons. When it is time, in God's time, we *will together* go play in the fields of the Lord."

> *See your self...* with enough discipline to receive the reward for extending kindness to all. And as this present lesson instructs us, there is no greater reward than peace.

January 30
Do Not Grow Weary

"Let us consider again today *the rule* of kindness. Do you grow weary already with this repetition? I hope this is not the case, for truly the Father's Will is our journey.

Love is the rule, and kindness and love are one.

The Path is oft times troublesome because you are unable to extend the simple act of kindness, and so through repetition the journey *will* become easier for all of us.

Do not grow weary, but come to Me and I will give you rest."

> *See your self...* accepting the rule of kindness as a daily happenstance, and if you become weary and perhaps unable to perform according to the Father's Perfect Plan, Jesus awaits to restore you to the Path. Go to Him, and He will provide both the rest and restoration that you need.

January 31
Walk Bravely Forward

"Good morning, My Children.

And yes, I say again, we take this journey together. You will hear much that bears repeating each day as we take these steps to Father, walking bravely forward in His Will.

Fear not. Be of good cheer."

> *See your self...* ending this month and walking bravely into the next, practicing Father's Will for kindness to one another. A "fear not" from our Brother Jesus means most definitely that these lessons offer absolutely nothing to us in the fear category.

FEBRUARY

February 1
In The Father's Will

"Have you not long sought the Father's Will for your life? Yes! And to remain in His Will is really not as difficult as some of you would believe.

He smiles upon the child who can simply love as He intends we love. Each day becomes easier, does it not? You awake and smile as you come to our little lesson book, as you receive these little lessons in truth. You are testing the waters even now, in trusting His Curriculum. And you know you have found the taste of peace most pleasant. Indeed, you are beginning to live in His Will.

Follow Me."

See your self... hand in hand with Jesus, coming eagerly now to the daily lessons. Ah, and wonder of wonders, your participation in this Heavenly Plan brings smiles to our Father's glorious Face.

February 2
You Do Well, My Children

"You delight our Father with every step you take on this journey to Him. The kindness rule is settling in now. A gentle reminder now and then is all you need. And we are happy to remind you until the thought to be kind to one another needs no more than the gentlest reminder before it becomes the rule and not the exception; and until peace becomes your life, until peace is all there is.

Yes, there will, indeed, be repetition until peace is the rule and not the exception.

Yes, your faith is tested, and often. But it grows strong with every passing day."

> *See your self...* moving steadily forward in the practice of the kindness rule. And you will also progress in peace never ending. Steady progress towards that peace is well worth any effort it entails.

February 3
What You Sow, So Shall You Reap

"Good morning, My children.

I have often given words to My children that concern "the garden." Songs have been written, poetry phrased, and I have oft been depicted as the Master Gardner.

Today we begin a new work together. We begin today to prepare for the crop of the future.

You are aware of the expression, "What you sow, so shall you reap." I want you to see that you have been sowing seeds of kindness and reaping peace.

Yes, in this garden in which we toil, this garden of both yours and My making, we found a product of our journey together.

And all of our work together now will concern itself totally with these few words of great truth, for indeed, "What you sow, so shall you reap."

> *See your self...* working side by side with the Master Gardner, sowing seeds of kindness and reaping a bumper crop of peace.

February 4
Tilling The Garden

"Do remember that we are in this work together. And today, as each day, we again begin a great work together, for we have seeds to sow that will one day bring to us a very great harvest.

We have been planting seeds of kindness. These are small seeds, but like the mustard seed, these seeds *will* produce a mighty harvest. You will see that as a great truth.

You need no more witness to the truth that kindness produces peace, than the evidence in your own life in just the past few days of our gardening together."

See your self... in an exercise of faith. You take the tiny proverbial mustard seed of kindness and you *will* see it produce peace beyond any measure of the peace you presently see possible.

February 5
Amazing Fruit

"You are about to bear some amazing fruit, My Brethren, but first we must prepare the garden soil.

We have work to do together. It is a new work, as I said, that requires a little labor – a kind of preparatory work.

We wish to create a very beautiful garden. Yes, a garden of great beauty, and the beauty we create must first consist of some heavy weeding.

We will begin with one question. Is there anyone today that you need to forgive?"

See your self... not forgiving someone, even your Self. And see the withholding of forgiveness as a weed. And yes, perhaps a weed with very deep roots requiring "some heavy weeding." Do it!

February 6
No Stone Unturned

"My children, when I asked you if there was anyone that you needed to forgive, many of you knew where there existed the weed of unforgiveness in your gardens.

Yes, lack of forgiveness will cause weeds, some *very deeply rooted* weeds that cause great spoiling of the terrain.

This will take some work. You already know that is truth. But as I have said before, we have plenty of time, for this is a time to be quiet together and to think ahead to the crops that we desire to plant.

Our seeds of loving-kindness will be sown throughout all our days together and they always drop into soil of great fertility and produce ever-bearing fruit, but we must always clear the garden bed of those weeds that do not bear good fruit and that choke out our seeds of goodness.

We will leave no stone unturned."

> *See your self...* searching your mind for any weeds of unforgiveness. "This *will* take some work." It's a worthy work or Jesus would not have directed us toward its undertaking. The seeds of loving-kindness *will* produce ever-bearing fruit.

February 7
Ever-Blooming Love

"Good Morning, My beloved children.

We will begin the weeding process today and we will remove one very deeply rooted weed at a time.

When I asked you if there is *anyone* you need to forgive, there were those who wondered at the question, for surely there *are* those among you who have worked on the task of removing *all* unforgiveness, and these children know that they, indeed, left no stone unturned.

You need to ask this question of yourself again. Is there anyone I need to forgive today?

And then we will go all the way down, step by step, through the process of removing every single root of unforgiveness; with the goal of a most magnificent garden that is, indeed, ever ever-blooming."

> *See your self...* fully accepting that unforgiveness is a weed, oft times, very deeply rooted and you personally doing *whatever it takes* to remove this grungy culprit robbing each of us from this promised magnificent garden of the ever ever-blooming variety.

February 8
We Will Come To Peace

"We embark on a journey of great excitement.

I told you before that the reward for our labor is peace. And how oft sought and yet elusive is peace. You have often wondered why it cannot be obtained with any consistency in your lives.

Now I tell you that step-by-step, lesson by lesson, we will come to peace. And it will be a peace unshakable by *any* circumstance.

That should excite you greatly, My children."

> *See your self...* in this very moment, greatly excited by the prospect of unshakable peace as the reward for each step and every lesson taken on this journey we take together, my brothers and sisters.

February 9
A Journey Of Great Delight

"I ask you now to be patient as we take this new step together. You need not fear, for we take a journey of great delight.

Oh, you will be troubled as we weed our gardens together. It is a troubling work sometimes. But each victory along the Path leads to joy. And joy is, indeed, the sister of peace; and yes, love, too.

This is the promise for the discipline of weeding diligently. Today we prepare the soil for the great harvest of the future."

> *See your self...* preparing the soil for the promised magnificent garden. Yes, disciplined enough for the daily work required, and ever conscious of His promised rewards for your continual diligence, peace and joy, and yes, love, too. Worthy, oh, so worthy is the Path we tread together in the Master's footsteps.

February 10
Set Every Captive Free

"I have come to liberate the spirit. We will work together to set every captive free. Hold no one prisoner to unforgiveness, My Children. Take no prisoners!

My children, I have said that we will set the captives free, and I ask you today, who are these captives we will free through forgiveness?

You are, My children! You are always the one held captive when you will not forgive one another. It is *you* then that we labor to free from misery to peace.

A worthy work, do you agree?"

> *See your self...* perhaps sifting the crevices of your memory banks this very day. Some buried unforgiveness

from long ago could come to mind with a little extra digging today. Do it! It's your own peace that is the reward for any effort it may take to free your Self from every semblance of unforgiveness. And yes, agree wholeheartedly with our Teacher. It is a worthy work!

February 11
Do You Obey Me?

"In just a few short days we have accomplished much work together. And we will accomplish so much more on our journey in the Father's Will.

We most certainly labor in the Father's Business when we extend kindness to all we meet on the Path. And you have taken My Words seriously into your thinking in these past days.

You are listening and you are putting your actions into high gear. You are laboring obediently in love. You are, indeed, doing as I say."

See your self... actively participating daily in the "Father's Business." Your continual expressions of kindness and ongoing forgiveness are the substance from which the *family business* grows. The success of the Family Business could very well be the Father's intent for all His children.

February 12
His Curriculum

"At first your steps are like that of an infant, halting and unstable. You fall often, yet you eagerly scramble to rise to the challenge for the call of adventure that lies ahead. You will soon be moving ahead, taking these steps in stride.

I tell you in truth that soon we will move briskly forward *together*. As you ponder forgiveness, mingle the command to forgive and set the captives free with your desire to perform acts of service, acts of kindness.

See the kindness you extend to one another as the extension of the Father's Love and see your Selves as His Ambassadors. Grow in the wisdom of His curriculum."

> *See your self...* perhaps for the very first time recognizing your kind acts and forgiving acts as service to the Father's Will to Love one another as He, Indeed, loves and forgives and is kind to each and every one of His children daily. Are we His Ambassadors of Love? Absolutely!

February 13
The Fertile Soil

"The fragrance of the fertile soil you plow reaches toward heaven as we prepare the garden for the Father's pleasure. A little work, a little planning, and we will soon present Him with an ever-blooming garden of great beauty."

> *See your self...* preparing and planning your own personal ever-blooming garden, filled to over flowing with acts of kindness and forgiveness. This magnificent garden is a present for our Father's pleasure. Oh, what joyful enterprises our gardens are becoming!

February 14
Love All My Children

"Today we simply continue our efforts on the Path. Yes, a review is very beneficial. You need to continue to be kind and to express your love to one another in this manner.

Smile at everyone you meet. Smile at the strangers, too, and the passersby, for are they not all your brothers and sisters on the journey? Yes, they are *all* My children. My love knows no limitations. Remember that we prepare for the great crop of the future."

See your self... with an ever ready smile today. A smile costs nothing, yet immeasurably blesses both the giver and receiver. How many smiles are possible today? Hopefully you place no limits on this easily given gift.

February 15
Dig Deeply

"The days grow longer as the season progresses.

You bring the Father great delight as we prepare and plan our gardens, pulling weeds of unforgiveness and plowing the soil. Press forward, always forward.

You are learning the lessons well. You have brought to mind many who needed the great kindness of your forgiveness.

There are some of your brothers and sisters who have left the physical realm, and they, too, may need the kindness, yes, the great practice of your forgiving mercy. Do not hold back.

Now you can begin to see the great areas of your thoughts that truly need the plowing, the breaking up of the rock-hard ground of aberrant thinking. Dig deeply, My children. It is necessary if you are to be truly free."

See your self... going back across the years to perhaps, an unforgiven parent or schoolmate whose unkind words still carry across the years with painful unforgotten memories.

Oh, this plowing and digging process to remove all the weeds is so necessary that the ever-blooming varieties we seek may grace every inch of space in these garden gifts we prepare for the Father of all grace and mercy.

February 16
Be Patient With One Another

"Today, My children, I ask you to be patient with one another. Patience is not an easy labor.

There is much in all your lives to test your patience. You have trials and you experience them often, for the Path we tread together is an uphill climb, with only little periods of rest along the way. Thus you must learn patience.

Patience is not a gift to be asked for. It is senseless to ask the Father for patience, for patience is gained *only* through trials, and who would ask for trials?

So today I ask you to be patient with one another, for there are many who have trials far greater than others. They need all the kindness you can muster."

> *See you self...* in this "uphill climb" side by side with the Master Gardener, patiently accepting the trials of life as the necessary fertilizer for our gardens. Are these then gardens of paradise? And could this ever-uphill climb be, indeed, a stairway to the promised heavenly paradise Kingdom within?

February 17
Islands Of Joy

"Notice that since we began, you have experienced little islands of joy in your days. You will experience these delightful moments more and more as we continue onward.

As you walk the Path today, there may be strangers you encounter. You do not know the heavy burdens that they may carry. And I will tell you that a tender smile, a gentle kindness, may do far more than you could ever know to lift their heavy burdens."

See your self... actually able to lift some brother or sister's burden with a smile. Will we find more "islands of joy" by the simple addition of more smiles in our busy days?

February 18
The Father's Business

"You may think that I have asked too little of you, My children. No! I ask you simply to be patient! These lessons *will* require more of you. The curriculum builds one step upon the other. And please remember, *never* will you be asked to give more than you are able.

Onward, My children! Each day has much for us to accomplish together. It is all the Father's Business. We do this for Him because He loves us, as I love you."

See your self... as a child loved by our Father and our older wiser Brother as well. The love commandment becomes easier to spread abroad throughout His entire Universe in the light of this amazing eternal love. He directs us onward, ever onward!

February 19
Serving The Father

"My children, see every part of your day as an opportunity to serve our Father. His Kingdom is all encompassing. No one lives outside His Domain.

Think today of *all* your actions as service to His Will. I know you have never thought deeply enough on the subject of His Will. And for many who *have* thought of themselves as seeking to find it, I will say that much that you see as ordinary circumstance is and has always been His Will.

Yes, it is *all* the Father's Business. And when I say all, I mean *all*. There is nowhere that God is not."

See your self…daily employed in service to the Father's Will. Yes, in everything you say and do as gainfully employed in the Father's Business. Can we ever consider any longer *anything* as ordinary circumstance after being so wondrously categorized by our Teacher?

February 20
Ordinary Circumstances

"Think of your ordinary labors, yes, the work you do each day. Your ordinary circumstances *are* His Will, and you would be much happier in this earthly experience if you could only look upon the ordinary with kindness.

Make the choice today to be happy. Yes, choose to be happy in your ordinary circumstances.

Smile upon yourself as you serve the Father in what many of you call "the daily grind," for then you could more easily see yourselves as laborers daily in His Will.

And by the simple choice of your will, a simple change in your thought life, you become instantly laborers in and for the Love of God."

See your self…changing your thoughts to a more positive frame of mind concerning the ordinary. And then perhaps, the words "take up your cross each day" take on a whole new meaning. And the ordinary becomes no longer a cross to bear. Now *see your Self*, living happily ever after in the Father's Will.

February 21
Daily Chores

"As you go about your daily services today, notice that most of the ordinary chores of your day are services to one another.

See them now as the Father's Will and serve Him with all the love you can muster for one another.

Then come to the end of this day in the knowledge that you have done these humble tasks for God.

You do well on this Path, My children, very well, indeed."

See your self... as a willing servant to our Father's Perfect Will as you go about your daily chores. Ah, and fully accept this truth from our Teacher that you do well on this ever-ascending Path.

February 22
The Path Seems Steep

"The Path seems steep sometimes, doesn't it, My children? Many times you feel unfulfilled and unrewarded.

I know how you feel. But be patient! The world *will* come to love.

You are making progress, and you know that is truth. It takes but an instant to call this meeting into existence. You are the one who chooses the time and the place. For indeed, My Brothers and Sisters, we are *always* ready to be in these *holy instants* with you. Rest a moment here with Me."

See your self... in simple obedience, resting just a moment longer in the Presence of our older, wiser Brother. And take His very encouraging words into the very essence of this day. "You *are* making progress!"

February 23
Will You Listen?

"Let us again talk about the reward for kindness. Be patient with My reminders for simple acts of kindness towards one another, for we seek together the reward for your repeated kindnesses, the steady continual growth in peace. We have spoken before of intermittent peace. You believe peace is intermittent because you see yourselves so often the victims of outer circumstances.

Were you to learn to handle all the outer circumstances with kindness, to all others as well as yourselves, you would not seem the victim any longer. You would see yourselves in the true light of that which you really are.

Rather than being reactors, reacting to the trials and tribulations of life, which are beset upon you, you would become My actors, acting on behalf of My truth.

You are the children of God! And you would see yourselves in His Image, the image that is only Love. But you must be willing to learn from Me.

Will you listen?"

*See your self...*with the required listening ear, tuned into the solutions to all your problematic trials and tribulations. Could the answer be so simple as acts of kindness to all concerned in life's unending difficulties?

February 24
Enduring Peace

"Today we take another step forward. We will grow in the ability to walk always in My peace.

You are not now walking continually in that peace that passes all human understanding. You are not walking in that peace which is unshaken by mortal circumstances. But such a state of mind and being is promised to those who love, as the Father would have you love.

Sit with Me and learn to feel My Presence, and I will bring you into enduring peace, for *I AM* the Prince of Peace, and I walk with you."

See your self... walking daily with the great I AM, the Prince of Peace Who promises you, His child, enduring peace. Is this then a promise worth both all your endeavors and indeed, worth waiting for?

February 25
Peace Is Your Portion

"My children, the gift of another day is here. It is a gift of goodness and, yes, great kindness. Each day presents the opportunity for growth.

I know you sometimes hesitate to extend kindness to all you meet, but does the task not grow easier with each passing day? And are you not also beginning now to see your daily work as service to our Father?

Ah, indeed you are learning to live in His Will and to walk in My Peace. As you begin to see all that surrounds you on your daily path as His perfect Will for your growth, you will find your step a little lighter on the path we tread together.

And is not peace your portion now with far more frequency than ever before? Of course it is! And so we take these forward, ever forward steps each day, hand in hand.

I AM with you."

See your self... in total acceptance of *all* in your daily walk as the perfect Will of our heavenly Father for your own personal growth. Accepting, allowing and surrendering to this Perfect Will is not always easy, but your growth is assured as you do exactly as He so desires.

February 26
Surrounded By Love

"As I have said before, you face the known and unknown, but knowing you are not alone allows you to walk fearlessly forward. You view the days with newfound courage and the unknown is no longer fearful.

This new lightness in your step causes you to walk in happy expectation. For the first time in your life there is an absolute knowing that you are always and ever surrounded by love, and you know, too, surprisingly, the definition of love itself has a new meaning for you.

This joy comes from knowing you are surrounded by the love of My Father."

> *See your self...* with this new lightness in your step. Yes, our Father ever surrounds you with His Love and thus you go forward each day fearlessly and with great courage. His boundless love is the great encouragement in *every* happening.

February 27
Bear No Grudge

"Over these past few weeks I have asked you to be kind to one another. There have been some brothers and sisters to whom it was surely easier to be kind to than others.

Were there not a few about whom you said, "No! I cannot be kind to that person? Yes, but know that when you refuse we understand that it is because you have been hurt; you have often been the victim of great cruelty. Father understands the difficulty that underlies your refusal to be kind, to forgive.

I would help you see that your refusal to be kind is bearing a grudge against another. These grudges are hard places in your thought life, yes, a stumbling stone, a rock that prevents the growth of blossoms in our gardens.

See every grudge as a great weed, for it surely is. You must labor to remove these grudges, one by one. You cannot have peace; you cannot walk in Father's Image if you bear a grudge against another.

Lay them *all* down and bring delight to our Father, Who *truly delights* to see His children walk in peace."

See your self...as servants to the Father's delight. How grand a thought that you might bring the Creator of All some measure of delight by laying down all grudges and walking in the peace that passes all understanding.

February 28
Difficult Lessons

"Yes, My children, I did say you are making progress. You do not see the progress as clearly as I do. You are so hard on yourselves!

You do not understand, as I do, that even those occasions of apparently taking backward steps, they are not backward steps at all. No! These harder steps are necessary. You need the difficult lessons as well as the ones that are easy; they are *all* programmed for your progress."

See your self...accepting all the lessons, difficult or of lesser difficulty, as simply the curriculum for your life experience. For the most part God's children are involved in a school-room experience rather than a play yard.

February 29
Much To Delight Us

"The season progresses and the day beckons with much to delight us. No task will be beyond our endurance for its fulfillment.

Step happily forward, for we progress in the service of Love. We have learned so very much together on the Path. We can step firmly forward with courage, for you now know with little doubt that I AM with you."

See your self ...as servants to the Love commandment. And never doubt Who walks with you in this blessed calling and that you are both courageous and capable of its fulfillment.

MARCH

March 1
Lay Your Burden Down

"I spoke to you of the Father's understanding of when you cannot immediately lay down the heavy burden of a grudge.

My children, you bring great delight to our Father when you walk in kindness and bear no grudges, He holds no one captive through unforgiveness. That kind of love is difficult for many of you to understand, for you hold in your mind *many* false images of the Father's true character.

In the days and weeks ahead we will lay aside *every* false image of the false god you have created. We will lay aside all delusions and only the truth will remain."

> *See your self...* fully accepting Father's full forgiveness of your every mistake. Ah, and this marvelous revelation remains absolutely clear. Father holds no grudges, absolutely none! Can we then do anything less than relinquishing all who might still remain in our own grudge bearing accounts?

March 2
Patient And Faithful

"You have so much to learn, My children. You will discover that I am not a hard taskmaster. I am patient and faithful to your commitment to these few minutes each day that we have set aside that I might teach you in the ways of our Father's Love.

We have a great distance to travel together, and there is much that will be truly exciting in our journey. I want to assure you today, that there is no hurry to complete any portion of the curriculum. We take each step slowly and there will be many lessons that we will faithfully review."

See your self... matching our Teacher's patient and faithful commitment to the curriculum for each day. Recognize that there is no need to hurry. His patience assures that in due time and yes, with some review, you *will* complete all the necessary curriculum.

March 3
A Very Able Gardener

"You have noticed that you cannot always complete a lesson on the day that you receive it. Sometimes you will struggle to complete an assignment. Many of the lessons will confront a weed with very deep roots in our garden. There will be times that you feel the weed has been removed only to discover the root was very deep and is still growing. That is certainly the way most often with the deep-rooted weeds of unforgiveness.

But worry not. You have in Me a very able Gardener, Who labors with you each day. We will do all the necessary weeding together. Our garden will bear amazing fruit."

See your self... removing from your thought life any semblance of worry over the lessons. Perhaps you have some

deep-rooted weeds of unforgiveness, but our Gardener
assures each of us that we labor together

March 4
Examine Anger

"Today, My children, I will ask you to examine anger, for you are often angry
at life's circumstances. And most often that anger is subconsciously with
you because, like the little child you really are, you cannot always have life
circumstances go according to your own way of thinking, according to the
way **you** think it should go. Yes, you are like a spoiled child in that regard.

I ask you now to simply lay down the sword, for all your angst is stabbing
away at your very own soul. You wound yourselves, My children."

*See your self...*laying down every sword of anger, whether
against your Self or any others. If anger wounds the soul,
it may very well, in like manner kill the body.

March 5
A Toxic Weed

"Is there one who has so grievously angered you that you feel you can never
forgive that person? Why has this happened? That is the question you must
ask. Ask it of Me.

Why did My servant Paul leave instructions to mankind, saying, "Do
not let the sun set on your anger?" Why indeed? Because he well knew that
the detrimental weed of anger could easily prevent any blossom from ever
bearing fruit.

Follow the counsel of your elder brother Paul and do not take today's
anger into tomorrow. Do not let the sun go down today until you release
all the captives, including yourselves. Go deeply into the soil of your

countenance and remove every root of bitterness that would spoil the beauty of these gardens that we so carefully prepare."

See your self... following Paul's advice and releasing everyone held captive by any anger you may have against anyone. Do it today! Anger is a weed that prevents ever-bearing fruit. Careful preparation is important in this ongoing process.

March 6
Be Happy!

"Let us labor to present to Our Father *all* He so richly deserves. He delights in His Children's happiness. Would you seek to rob Him of His Delight today? Of course not! Let us do all that is necessary to bring Him delight. Let us labor joyously and unceasingly in His Love.

Be happy! Yes, you can do this! You can begin today to be happy. And if you can be happy for just a little while today, by some simple acts of kindness, especially to yourselves, then we can extend that happiness into tomorrow, and then into *all* our tomorrows.

I do not ask for more than you can give."

*See your self...*accepting the promise that you might delight our Father thru your happiness and then elaborate on the possibility of bringing Him continual delight by your attention to your own happiness. Selfish? Indeed, not! Begin today to do all you can do to bring happiness into "*all* our tomorrows."

March 7
Let Go Of Unhappiness

"Release your anger! Release your bitter thoughts! My children, simply let them all go – these thoughts that keep you captive to unhappiness. Do you want to be happy? O course you do! And so why would you let unforgiveness stand in the way of what you seek?

Yes, My children, happiness is a choice. You can choose this day to remain captive to all your negative thoughts or you can simply say, "No!" to all that would rob you of your joy. You do not fully realize the freedom that is really yours. What a powerful tool you have in God's gift to you of free will!

Yes, the great beauty of this earth experience is that you are all free will creatures. You *can* decide how you feel. Choose to be happy."

See your self... this very day, making the choice for happiness. Your feelings are your choice. Choose wisely.

March 8
Choose Happiness

"You already know that you are free to choose between right and wrong. But how often do you feel you have chosen the wrong over the right? We will not dwell on that today. No! We will dwell on your freedom of choice for happiness.

And why would you ever choose otherwise? Why Indeed! I will tell you why. You are creatures of habit. Day after day many of you choose to spend the majority of the gift of your days in bitterness and unforgiveness. Oh, you may deny that the majority of your days are spent this way, but you lie to yourselves often. You pretend to be happy. But is that the truth?

Choose to be happy! Think on that today, My children, as we work. You can choose happiness. It is easier than the alternative, of this you can be sure."

See your self...taking the time this very day to "choose to be happy." It *is* the easier choice, "of this you can be sure," very sure indeed!

March 9
Remove The Barriers

"I tell you to choose happiness. And if it is difficult for you to be happy, and just as difficult to remain in constant peace, then something needs to be discussed. Yes, we need to begin some serious lessons together.

You need not worry. Peace and happiness will come. In the days and weeks ahead, we will work *together* to remove every barrier to peace and happiness. And we will, by the removal of these barriers, bring great delight to our Father, and very great delight to ourselves."

See your self...doing the necessary work to remove every single barrier to your own personal peace and happiness and thus while making this concentrated effort you will bring great delight to our Father. Whatever it takes, you can do it!

March 10
The Key To Forgiveness

"The barrier to peace and happiness is unforgiveness. Now, again I ask you, My children, to forgive one another, as you *all* have received forgiveness. To remain angry day after day with one who has wronged you makes you captive and not the other. Think this thru.

You dwell on your wounds, and that dwelling is the same as rubbing broken glass repeatedly across a major injury. Will that injury ever heal with the constant re-wounding? Never! Healing will never come with constant irritation.

Let it all go. Freedom comes to those who remove all unforgiveness. It is a worthy labor. Begin today!"

See your self...as forgiven of all your mistakes and take no one captive to their mistakes in your own regard. Father generously forgives all mistakes. Can His children do anything less than follow His amazing example for gracious living? If peace on earth is ever to come, then no captives to unforgiveness must remain in Father's earthly domain.

March 11
Each Day Is A Gift

"Begin today with a new way to live. Each day is a gift.

Do you remember chalk and blackboards from your early school days? At the end of every day, the boards were erased so that the following day the surfaces would be clean to begin again – as a beautiful new day with a clean slate to start anew the lessons to be learned.

Bring nothing negative into the new days. Forget any hurts. Forget the little nicks and pains from the day before. They are gone. Face the new day with a new lightness in your step and kindness in your heart."

See your self...in the gift of this new day taking a mental eraser to the blackboard of your mind and erasing any unforgiveness from the day before. And wouldn't it be a good idea to make a mental note to a morning-by- morning erasure of any negative influence from any previous day?

March 12
His Perfect Image

"You have a Friend Who goes with you today, Who takes your hand. Of this you can be very sure. I love you with an everlasting Love. All that lies ahead we face *together*.

The lessons will grow easier. You will learn to love in the Father's Name. You will show forth the eternally glowing light of His Perfect Image. Yes, you will show forth His Image to all that go with you on this Path."

See your self... more aware of Who takes your hand each day. You are not alone in all of life's lessons. All that is ahead on the Path you face "together." How good is that?

March 13
Walk In The Light

"And what is the Image of the Father? You know Him as Love. What does Love look like? He wears a beautiful Robe of Love. It is a coat of many colors, and its predominant color is forgiveness.

He holds no one captive. Not one of His children does He hold in the captivity of unforgiveness. Each of you walk *daily* in forgiveness. He never takes one grudge from one day into another. And that is Light, My children.

And what is darkness? You know the answer. Those who walk in unforgiveness, walk, indeed, in the darkness, and they daily stumble on the Path.

Would you walk in His Image? Then you would take no grudge from this day into another. These lessons are not as difficult as some of you may think. It is far easier to walk in the light then to stumble in the darkness."

See your self... refusing to bear grudges any longer. Wrap the Father's Robe of forgiveness on your very own shoulders before you take one more step into the gift of this beautiful day.

March 14
Lamplighters

"The people who walked in darkness have seen a great light." Yes, many have seen the light. They know the Love Light of our Father beckons them to walk in His Image. But seeing and doing are quite different in the performance. You know this is truth.

You are called to be light, which is the essence of Love, My Brothers and Sisters. You are Ambassadors of His Love and Love has an obligation to show forth, as lamps show forth the light to show the way through the dark.

You can do as I did. I told you that you are, indeed, "the light of the world." You are His Lamplighters. Not only are you to shine but also you can light other lights by your love. And one day all of this Universe will be the glowing diamond of our wondrous creation."

See your self... as His Lamplighter. Will you show forth His Love this very day? Accept this role as an Ambassador in His Service. Every loving act leads this Universe to its "glowing diamond" status.

March 15
Divine Kilowatts

"You feel you have just a small light, one that flickers, and oft time you think it has gone almost completely dark. No! One little kindness and the flicker greatly broadens and illumines.

Let these words today encourage you, My dear Ones. Every effort leads to more "divine kilowatts" for brighter days for yourselves and those who walk with you."

See your self... raising your "kilowatts" by more kindness today. Surely you can find someone whose path could use a little brightening power. Perhaps kindness even to your Self might factor into a truly "divine kilowatt" day.

March 16
Let Your Light Shine!

"My children, do not think that your little efforts to shine forth His Love ever go unnoticed. For if He is aware of every sparrow, He knows your little acts of kindness on behalf of Him. He knows and *loves* each and every effort. Shine! Walk on, in His Love."

See your self...shining ever more brightly in your concentrated and yes, consecrated efforts to walk daily in His amazing, *never* ending Love.

March 17
Say No To Darkness

"Saying no to darkness is not an easy task. But, My children, if our gardens are to bloom in love and light, then *every* weed of negativity must be removed. You already know how difficult that can be.

Negativity is a habit; it is also a choice. See for yourself that dark thinking is a choice, yet there is truly only light. Understand that this is truth and we can begin the necessary work. I will work with you.

I have told you before that happiness is a choice. You may always choose between happiness and the alternatives. See happiness first as positive and the alternatives as negative and you will understand why it is necessary to set all the captives free.

There is a great deal of labor for all of us if you are to be free, as Father would have you be. Understand that principle, and we can begin the necessary lessons."

*See you self…*accepting the task of breaking perhaps a long standing habit of negative thinking. Negative thinking is your personal joy robber. Offer no resistance to this principle and fully understand that Jesus goes with you into every day and every lesson. Who else do you need to help you with these challenges? Who, Indeed!

March 18
Let Us Begin With You

"I am with you every step of the way. I do walk the entire Path with you. And the Father's Business is to bring His Universe to Love. It is only mankind's negative thinking that stands in the way.

Let us take another look at the gift of today as a place to take some major steps forward in the restoration of His Kingdom to His full Intent. And let us begin today with you.

Put a guard on the doorway of your mind. You are the captive of your thinking. You can choose today to serve love and light and it is a very worthy service."

See your self… as one of God's free will children able by choice to guard the doorway to your mind. The choice is yours for every thought that goes through that doorway. Bar all that is negative. Choose only Love. One day the loving Universe of His full Intent will come.

March 19
No Sabbath Rest

"I call you, My children, to His Service in Love and if you are truly My disciples, this service is an easy labor. Do you see yourselves today as truly His Children? Then let us do some serious gardening today.

Gardening in His Vineyard is ongoing. There is no Sabbath rest from Love. There is no day of rest from the labor of seriously loving one another. You must seek to serve *daily* in His Will. And His Will *is* that you love one another. You can *never* say no to Love as Kingdom dwellers, however difficult it may seem."

> *See your self*...as a disciple in service to no other King or Kingdom than His. Loving one another is His Will. And service to His Will then is your will also. Love as He would have you love.

March 20
Garments Of Love

"Put on the garments of love as you arise each morning. Say these words each morning as you set your foot upon His Path. "I will love in His wonderful Name. I will love in the Father's Will and His Way. His Name is wonderful. His Name is Love."

How then, My children, do you love in His Will and His Way? Be kind to one another. There it is again, in all its simplicity. Simple acts of Kindness. Say no words of malice. Refrain from gossip. Do harm to no one. This is truly the Father's Will and His Way."

> *See your self*...following this Path of very great simplicity. Be kind. Refrain from gossip and all malice and above all harm no one. Live and love as He wills you to live and love.

March 21
You Will Reap Peace

"Yes, you know this is the truth. Refrain from malicious actions as well as negative thoughts and you will sow peace. My disciples are truly diligent in their thoughts as well as their actions.

You wonder at the feasibility of gardening in your *thoughts* as well as your actions. Wonder no longer, My children, for this is truly our curriculum. Love one another, in thoughts and in deeds.

Day in and day out be laborers in His Love and you *will* reap peace. Yes, you will reap peace in *all* its fruitful abundance."

*See your self...*accepting this guarantee of fruitful abundance as you labor in His Service of Love. You will absolutely reap what you sow.

March 22
Guard Your Thoughts

"On this day, My children, we will begin a serious study on our thought life, for it is within our thoughts that the lack of peace begins or where peace is birthed.

You *must* spend time learning the habit to guard your thoughts. You wonder at this. You have thousands of random thoughts in every hour; and yes, you have often thought yourselves captive to your thoughts, or a victim.

But, no, you have a choice to say no to all that would spoil the fruit of peace.

This is not an easy gardening task, of that you can be sure. But the result is oh so very worth the effort involved."

*See your self...*placing a guard at the doorway to your mind, allowing nothing of a negative nature to enter therein.

Begin today to think of your mind as *sacred* ground. The reward for diligence is peace.

March 23
Transformation Of Thinking

"I have told you that each day is a beautiful gift, and it is. But you often bring with you into the new day the garbage from the day before. A transformation of thinking is necessary. It is a slow process.

You have disciplined your selves to meet each day with Me, My children. You have traveled through the past weeks of lessons and you are still with Me. Why? Because you have seen small steps of progress!

No task will be beyond endurance for its fulfillment. Step happily forward. You know I will guide you. Trust Me to give you the Answers. I will help you transform your thinking."

> *See your self...*following His directions and step *happily* into today. You are making progress! And if the remembrance of some "trash" from yesterday should enter your mind, say NO! You are, after all, establishing sacred mental ground. You are not a garbage collector.

March 24
Continue The Progress

"You *will* continue the progress. You desire to love in the Father's Will and His Way. And those little moments, yes, little seeds of Peace have made you desire to harvest a full and abundant crop. You will continue. And you will learn to *discipline* your thought life.

Is there a weed from yesterday? Have you opened your eyes today with a burden from the past? It can be removed by a simple act of will. Say no!

Did you fail to love? Then do what is necessary today: whatever is necessary, to not take the weed into tomorrow. It may take a little labor, but it is the Father's Will that you be free."

See your self... living one day in total peace. Whatever it takes, do it! Would you weed a physical garden then pile the weeds on your kitchen floor to decompose? Absolutely not! Get rid of every trashy mental weed. This garden we prepare *is* sacred.

March 25
Walk This Day In Peace

"I wish to walk this day in peace and love." Of course, you do! Say it again, My children, "I wish to walk this day in peace and love."

When I ask you to forgive one another and you notice in your thinking one whom you cannot forgive, this is the source of your anger and unrest. You believe your anger is justified. You say you are angry for just cause, but in truth you are unnecessarily punishing yourselves. And your unrest touches everyone around you.

To walk in peace is a choice. Peace depends on you. And if it is your true desire, it will happen. It is that simple.

Can you not take these simple little words, write them down and put them in a place that your eyes will fall upon often? The refrigerator door is a good place, or perhaps in a most visible place in your bathroom.

Then throughout the day, your eyes will remind your minds of the curriculum before us."

See your self... making a serious effort to walk this day in peace. Follow the suggestion and place the words "I *will* walk this day in peace and love" in some prominent place for your eyes to fall upon often. Sometimes a little reminder is all we need.

March 26
Will To Walk in Peace

"You can learn to love and also walk in total peace. Of course, it is an act of will. It is your choice. And remember *always* that you are all free will children.

Choose today to serve Him in love, and peace will be the reward of your disciplines. Discipline your thought life, My children. Peace is the reward of that discipline.

You have the habit of nursing negative thoughts. Like feeding a child with sour milk, you nurse all the negativity of the past. And I say, do not feed anything negative into your thought life, for all negativity will surely spoil our gardens.

Negative thinking is counter-productive to love. And it is the Love lessons that we must learn. Learning to Love is the curriculum."

*See your self...*embracing the Love curriculum with all your heart, mind and strength. Be ever on guard for the weeds of negativity, for surely they spoil the garden of our Father's holy and wise Intent. Let His Intention be our will.

March 27
Our Little Victories

"Give your selves credit today for the forward steps we have taken together. There is some mystery, of course, but our disciplines are our little victories that spur us onward.

Are we not pleased with the victories? Yes! And there are many places to love each day. You no longer turn away from them.

Did I not say the journey would grow easier?"

See your self...giving your Self credit for the forward steps. This journey takes discipline. And there is a promise that the journey *will* grow easier. Onward!

March 28
This Beautiful Day

"Today is a beautiful gift. Is your Path ahead clear? Pause a moment. Is there anyone you need to forgive? If so, then simply do it! Take no burdens into this beautiful day. It is as simple as saying "I forgive."

Do you remember Me saying, "Father, forgive them for they do not understand what they are doing?"

Few can seriously understand when they kill love. Yes, there are those who murder love daily with their unkind and thoughtless words and actions. But we are no longer in that witless circle. We are *beginning to see*, as Father would have us see."

See your self...as no longer a part of that "witless circle" of Father's children, who murder love with words and actions. You have a beautiful garden to maintain. Take the time, if needed, for some mental weeding as our Master suggests.

March 29
Face Each Day In Freedom

"If we will give some conscious thought at the beginning of each day to forgiveness, we can face each day in total freedom. Take a moment to examine the garden of your thought life. A stray weed of unforgiveness here or there will spoil the day. We cast it from us with an act of will, and then step forward happily today.

Now then see how much love you can cast about.

Yes, cast your love into today and see the manifold return. All that remains in the tasks ahead is our diligence to His Will."

See your self...daily giving conscious effort to removing every weed of unforgiveness. Then you will know how well your garden grows, indeed, overflowing with love and joy, great peace and happiness.

March 30
Sowing And Reaping

"How much love did you take into yesterday? A simple smile, a favor given, a kind word here and there? All are seeds of Love, My children, and soon you will see some blossoms in our gardens. Following the blossoms come the fruit. You will see fruit that is ever blooming. And you will know the truth that life is ever sowing and reaping. Sow love and you *will* reap love."

See your self...smiling more often. Think of your smile as a gift of love, perhaps to someone today who really needs your smile. And assuredly some smiles will come smiling back at you.

March 31
We Do Advance

"For many of My children, the command to love is not an easy task. You have been hurt often and some of you live lives at the scene of a murdered love.

Love begins as a tender seed. It needs nurturing to grow. And many of you tried and failed at the nurturing task. And the failures have made you fearful, frightened to give your love again. But Love is truly an endless bounty."

See your self...tapping into Love's endless supply, and ever ready to give to both your Self and all those who surround you. Yes, indeed, "Love your neighbor as your Self."

APRIL

April 1
Seventy Times Seven

"I have given you some words for you to remember daily. When asked by Peter how often you must forgive, these words should be remembered; "seventy times seven." That means you must forgive without ceasing, for truly that is an example of the Father's Image. He would have you forgive as He forgives. Forgive all!

Does that mean that you must remain in endless situations of pain and suffering? Not at all! It means you must forgive. Not for the sake of those who murdered love, but for the sake of your selves who bear the wounds and, yes, scars of the murder.

And there are those who cry for release from the graveyards of your making. These are heavy words this morning. Some of the lessons are not always easy. Do not expect always words of exhortation that tickle the ears."

*See your self...*beginning this new month with renewed enthusiasm for the journey. The lessons are not always easy. Some you will always find challenging. Ah, but the ever-bearing fruit in our gardens is well worth any labor these lessons entail. Forgive all and release your Self from all your own mental graveyards.

April 2
Accept A Gold Star

"You do well, My children, with the weeding of your gardens. But there are bitter roots of unforgiveness still, and these roots grow deep. Before you leave our little morning classroom, be sure that every visible weed is pulled.

Then go happily into today, like little children at recess, and accept a gold star in today's curriculum. One day at a time, a gold star here and there and, yes, we do advance."

See your self... fully delighted with today's gold star and happily looking forward to all the gold stars in your future.

April 3
The Major Curriculum

"You wonder on occasion if you truly do advance. I say to you, you do! But you cannot always measure the advancement, for you focus far too much on your errors. I assure you, you are listening and you are learning.

Perhaps you have noticed lately that there are many opportunities for kindness and a tender word, where once anger was your quick retort.

And you are often asking the question, "Is there anyone I need to forgive?" You are remembering quickly to forgive and discovering how much pain comes into the world with each mindless act of thoughtlessness. It is much easier to stop anger before the wounds occur.

To love one another is the major curriculum. Be kind. Be gentle. Be gentle at every opportunity."

See your self... growing daily in kindness and gentleness, especially in the area of tongue control. A kinder and more gentle speech is evolving that befits the children of Father's heavenly Kingdom on earth.

April 4
Swords Into Plowshares

"Scripture teaches you to "beat your swords into plowshares." A plowshare is a mighty gardening tool, is it not? Put your swords away. The attack of the tongue has murdered more than *all* the bombs and tanks and cannons from every century. Guard the tongue! Stop the wounding! Let gentle words flow freely."

See your self...putting a mental chain across the doorway of your mouth. Try, really try, to never again wound a brother or sister with words of anger or malicious unkindness.

April 5
Love Is Gentle

"Be gentle Lovers, My children. Do you find gentleness new to your thinking? Love *is* gentle.

Will you make room in your garden today for seeds of gentleness? Ah, these tiny seeds will produce ever-blooming fruit.

You are loved, My children, with a love far beyond your human understanding.

It is a gentle love, and yes, most kind. And this love that flows from our Father to you finds its greatest expression through you.

He can use your lips today to express His Love. He can use you, each of you, to sow the seeds of love today."

See your self...allowing our Father to use your lips today and even more. Let Him use all of you as the human dispenser of His Amazing Love. Focus on your Self as His channel. Let every one of us be about our Father's most worthy Business.

April 6
His Gentle Touch

"You say, "What can I do to serve our Father?" Answer His Call to love one another. Be kind. Be gentle.

There will be an opportunity this very day, to serve in His Name.

He has little children everywhere on this planet today who need to feel His tender Touch. And He truly sends you forth to administer His Love.

Smile often and see His Smile returned. Let your touch be in keeping with His gentle Touch and Love *will* flow back.

Give your happiness away and see it returned in manifold ways. Go in His Love for He does send you."

> *See your self*...serving our Father by answering His Call to love one another. Your kindness and gentleness to all our brothers and sisters is the sacred emblem of your high calling.

April 7
His Name Is Love

"His Name is wonderful! His Name is Love! And our Father does call you, My children, into His Service as Lovers. Each and every day, see yourselves as servants of His Love.

Some days are easier than others. Some days you must turn the other check. You must pull the weed of unforgiveness. You must be diligent to the weeding process in these gardens *we* prepare.

Yes, you are loved. Cast that love forth and you *will* see the fruit of all the seeds you sow."

> *See your self*...recognizing Who it is that prepares the garden with you every time you see that little pronoun "we."

You are not alone in this great garden effort. And you *will* see fruit for *every* seed you sow.

April 8
Father Would Have You Dream

"You know your thoughts can be the springboard for an abundant crop of ever-blooming blossoms. You have dreams of love returning now. You dream as Father would have you dream. You "see" with vision for the days when the paradise of His intent becomes the garden of your sowing.

And so, as the weeding continues, you labor in the preparation of the soil that will produce the garden of your dreams. You guard daily the random sowing of the weeds of malice and discontent. Your willful seeds of anger are no longer cast randomly about.

You catch your self often, holding your tongue. You wish to harm no one. You think before you speak. It is easier now to be cautious.

With Him, all things are possible. Your dreams and *Mine* will come true."

See your self...daily monitoring your thoughts and actions in alignment with the Father's Vision for the paradise of His Intention. The Master Gardener, Who gardens with you, shares the same vision. Our dreams for His Paradise *will* come true garden by garden.

April 9
Choose Love!

"My servant, Paul, gave this key to positive thinking centuries ago when he said, "Whatsoever is pure and honest and true, think on these things." He called his brothers and sisters away from negative thinking. He called the servants of God to thoughts of purity, honesty and truth and that call remains the same today. The call to positive thinking is timeless.

Today I ask you to simply put a guard at the doorway of your thinking. Again, I ask you to say *no* to negativity. You can simply realize that you are not a slave to negativity. Negative thinking is not simple random happenstance! You may direct your thoughts on *any* path of your choice.

Choose Love! It is after all, the Father's Will."

See your self...guarding the doorway of your thinking, and no more in slavery to negativity. Choose wisely to walk in the Father's Will for positive mental choices. Why choose any path other than His? Why, Indeed!

April 10
Our Lessons Bear Repeating

"Does it seem, My children, that our lessons are repetitious? They do bear repeating, and often, for you learn by repetition. Do you remember how you learned mathematics and spelling as children? You repeated the lessons over and over again. You still learn in the same manner.

I ask you to view today as the beautiful gift it is. Today is like a garden. I ask you to plant Love, with a hand filled to overflowing with Our Father's Love. Cast about all the seeds of love that it is possible for you to plant today; for *every* seed will bear fruit, of that you can be sure."

See your self...casting all your love seeds into the beautiful garden of today. How abundantly you have received our Father's Love, forever flowing into your own life. Now simply keep the flow going.

April 11
Give Yourself A Smile

"Are you happy today, My children? If the answer is yes, be kind, and take a ready smile with you into today.

And would you give yourself a smile? Smile now as you read these words. See, even the thought of smiling can give an uplifted attitude.

Do you need to practice smiling? No! Smile often. It can be an amazing gift you bring into your day. Yes, smile often, for it almost always brings an instant return."

See your self...smiling often today. And see your smile as an "amazing gift," costing absolutely nothing, yet perhaps bringing sunshine into a brother or sister's un-sun-shiny day.

April 12
His Children's Happiness

"Now let Me ask you again if you are happy. And I will say today that if you are not, the problem of your unhappiness *always* comes from a weed-filled thought life. Get to work to change your weedy thinking.

You can be sure if you are unhappy, there is a weed with roots growing below the surface. Unhappiness has its root in unforgiveness.

Place this thought in the garden of your thinking. Father delights in His children's happiness. Have you ever thought of something you could personally do that would bring delight to God? You *can* delight Him *often* by planting seeds of Love. How many can you plant today?"

See your self...stepping into today with the intent to plant some seeds of Love. And every one you plant *will* bring delight to our Heavenly Father.

April 13
Clear The Path For Happiness

"Do the work and bring delight to our Father. And I will tell you now, that even the labor involved brings Him delight.

Yes, weed pulling makes a clear statement of your intent to labor in the Father's Will. He knows how difficult sometimes it is to forgive. He knows the pain and sufferings of your lifetime.

Let us look to the Father. Does He ever move away from giving His Love? Does He withhold His Love from any of His children? Never! And if you believe He does, then you do not know Him as I do.

Every act of forgivenenss clears the Path for happiness. And the effort of your labor will produce abundant fruit, of that you may be very certain.

Meanwhile, continue to weed wherever and whenever weeding is needed. And always try to remember to think before you speak."

See your self...putting today's suggestion to "think before you speak" into practice. Perhaps a little note placed strategically would remind you of such a worthy practice.

April 14
Seeds Of Compassion

"Now let me speak to you of compassion. When you forgive, the seeds of compassion take root in our gardens. Father is compassionate. He forgives *all*. And you strive to become the Children of His Image, do you not? Of course, that is our daily intent.

And so today think of yourselves as students in a course centered on compassion; and as you think, so shall you become.

You will follow in the Father's Footsteps. Love is compassionate. And I will tell you again, today, that God is Love and you are Love. Be prepared to hear these words often, My children. You are Love."

*See your self...*in every compassionate action as an extension of the Father's Love. Be good students of the Love curriculum. It is a Course you can master.

April 15
Each Day Is A New Beginning

"My beloveds, why do you struggle to believe My Words, "You are Love"? You struggle against this because you have not forgiven yourself your many *supposed* errors.

Yes, you have made many unwise decisions in your lifetime. You have acted without understanding the consequences of your actions. You hold yourself accountable for your inability to understand, and in so doing, you retain guilt, and this guilt has placed a chain across the doorway to your happiness.

Loose the chain! You are not held accountable. Father keeps no record. He understands fully your inability to understand."

*See your self...*forgiving your Self from the countless errors against your Self as well as all others. Is it true that Father keeps no record or the errors? Absolutely! Then can you follow His Perfect Example today?

April 16
Father Has Forgiven You

"My children, I spoke a great truth, and the records of the centuries bear evidence of My Words: "Father, forgive them for they know not what they do." In truth, My children, you rarely understand your mistakes. I ask you today to leave behind *all* the errors of your yesterdays.

This bears some understanding. Simply begin by accepting that Love understands. God understands. His Love is immense.

Forgive yourself this morning. Wash all the past away with the simple thought that Father has forgiven you *completely*. And a new day is here and the slate is clean. Each day is a new beginning."

> *See your self*...accepting the importance of this very great truth. Through God's amazing grace on your behalf, your forgiveness is complete. Yes, leave behind all the errors of all your yesterdays. The slate *is* clean and today you have a whole new beginning.

April 17
Each Day A New Beginning

"I want you to concentrate fully now on the words, "each day is a new beginning." Stop for just a moment and repeat these words slowly. "Each day a new beginning." Concentrate on this one fact. Live today, one moment at a time.

You and I are *together* right now. And we will stay together through every moment of this day, and I will stay with you in every moment of every today. Each day is a new beginning of a new adventure with Me."

> *See your self*...together with this Friend in all the moments of every day. And freely accept the greatest gift in the adventure of this new day's experience is this inimitable Friendship.

April 18
God Is In The Mystery

"Each day has its share of mystery, of the unforeseen. But you do have a Friend Who faces all the unforeseen with you. You will understand this truth more and more as we progress together.

And this incredible truth bears repeating. You do have a Friend Who faces all the unforeseen with you.

There is absolutely nothing to fear. Together we can and will accomplish everything that needs to be accomplished. I take your hand each day. We walk the Path together and thus will it ever be.

Enjoy today! It's a very important day in our Father's grand Plan. For indeed, every day is a holy part of His Perfection!"

> *See your self...*in partnership with a Friend Who will go every step of the way with you. Hand in hand all can and will be accomplished. You may rest assured in the perfection of Father's Perfect Plan. And be equally assured in the perfection of the Partner Who shares this great adventure with you.

April 19
I take Your Hand Each Day

"I take your hand each day. And this is no idle fantasy. I tell you the truth. You are not alone. There is no need for any apprehension about anything whatsoever. We have been though many hardships together. The hardships *are* the lessons. The curriculum is designed for each of you individually, and is, in its entirety, for the Father's purpose; for your growth in His Kingdom Principles.

The lessons are sometimes very difficult, for there is no growth without adversity. There is a saying, "No pain. No gain." You understand this, do you not? It is in trial and adversity that your character takes form."

> *See your self...*in every trial and every adversity, as growing in our Father's Kingdom Principles and taking the necessary steps toward your own personal character growth.

April 20
Place Your Trust In Me

"You need not fear the future, nor do you need to know anything about it. Trust Me *fully*. The Plan for your Path is perfect, of that you can be very sure.

You are *exactly* where you need to be right now. You are *always* in His Will. That may not seem to be the truth, especially for those of you who walk in pain in the moments of this day.

Some of your present pain may be from your choosing, from the choices of your faulty thought life. We will work together on the release of this pain in the days and weeks ahead. But for now let us concentrate on this day alone. Let us see how much love you can bring into today."

See your self…first and foremost, loving your Self by releasing the pain and guilt from your errors and mistakes. The lessons to be learned are in the errors and mistakes. Even your supposed failures are in Our Father's Will. Learn well the lessons, loving your Self every step of the way on the great adventure you and He take together.

April 21
Live By The Rules Of Love

"You know some of the rules already. Be kind. Be gentle. Think before you speak. Plant the seeds of love, and the fruit of love will do much to remove the sadness that has caused your pain, and yes, your tears.

Also take a moment now to remember the forgiveness rule before you step into today. There is no need to take unnecessary pain or sadness into the beautiful gift of now.

Review the rules of love daily and the Path will be far easier to tread, My beloveds. Give no thought for tomorrow. Today will keep us very busy in our Father's Business."

See your self...employed daily in the Father's Business. His Business is Love. You can find no better employment in the Universe. Live by the rules. Plant the seeds and reap the harvest. It's that simple.

April 22
The Important Universal Principle

"I return your thinking today to review the *important* principle to forgive one another.

You need to be reminded often, for you habituate unforgiveness. You are far too judgmental of your brothers' and sisters' failures. You set far too high a standard upon them; one that you have great difficulty living up to yourselves.

Relax your standards. No! I do not ask you to be tolerant of the actions that are hurtful. But I do ask you to forgive these actions when they occur. All children learn from their errors and mistakes. It is a difficult way to evolve, but nonetheless, this is the way that civilizations advance, a step-by-step process.

Ah, but you *are advancing* beautifully, of that you can be very sure."

See your self... accepting this compliment from the Teacher Himself. "You are advancing beautifully" in this step-by-step, one-day at a time process. Onward! You can do whatever it takes.

April 23
Your Thought Life

"We enter now into a new phase of our curriculum. We will go day-by-day together in the lesson plan working again in your thought life. Why? Simply because *all* mankind's thinking needs correcting! And we begin with you.

Come with Me each day and see how very much we can accomplish together. Step by step we go, and always hand in hand."

See your self...taking the time each day to think about your thoughts. Understand that there are areas that need correction and be happy to make any necessary adjustments. Clearly see that "stinkin' thinkin" is not an option in our curriculum.

April 24
The Perfection Of His Plan

"The Path is planned for you each day. Before you open your eyes each morning, the Path is there.

The Father has your lessons outlined. Accept the perfection of His Plan. Simply understand this one truth about the Father's Will. It is all our Father's Will.

I have heard every one of your rebuttal questions before. Is sickness His Will? Is death His Will? Does He want your husband of your wife to get cancer and die too soon? Is war His Will? And the questions go on and on. No! Listen again.

Nothing is outside His Sight. He allows everything. But think how much of all these things are humanity's will. Be careful how you phrase your questions. How many of the problems of the earth experience are from mankind's machinations and not from God's?

You see what trouble you enter into when you follow the lines of your own thinking, instead of allowing your mind to align with Mine.

Thus until you can think as I do, and as the Father would will for us to do so, these are mankind's lessons to learn; yes, mankind's problems to solve, and all under the curriculum heading of free will choice. I *will* help you."

See your self...carefully reading the words of this great and very wise teaching. Free will has, indeed, maximized mankind's problems. And you so often fall into the faulty thinking category. He *will* help you align your thinking with our Father's Perfect Will.

April 25
Sometimes You Feel So Alone

"Sometimes you feel so alone, My Beloveds. But this is not the truth. You are *never* alone. I have told you that I will never leave you nor forsake you. It is you who feel the separation and this feeling is false.

You often feel separated from My love because of guilt. You have not disappointed our Father, although you have often disappointed your Self, and thus you withdraw from Him. He *never* withdraws from you."

*See your self...*releasing every thought of disappointing our Father. He loves you always and He never withdraws that love from you. Your feelings to the contrary are simply not the truth.

April 26
God's Love Is Unconditional

"You must learn a new lesson now about the Father's Love. His Love in not dependent on conditions; He is not a conditional lover as is mankind's tendency. His Love is not dependent on whether you are good or bad. That is a great myth that you must put to the test.

Our Father *is* Love, and His Love is not conditional. Learn this lesson well, My beloveds. Learn this lesson well!"

*See your self...*erasing the image of our Father as some kind of Santa Claus character… making a list and checking it twice. Gonna find out who is naughty or nice. No toys for the naughty ones. Erase that image forever. Our Father is *not* Santa Claus…in no way, shape or form.

April 27
Break The Cycle

"My beloveds, as difficult as it is for you to learn and fully understand that Father is not a conditional lover, *it is necessary* for you to learn to love unconditionally.

From early childhood, you have been rewarded for good and punished for error. This teaches conditional loving. And you take this teaching into every area of your life experience. It has taught you that you punish your own children in like manner. If they do something that displeases you, you simply withdraw your love and the cycle goes round and round. We now begin a labor to stop the cycle."

See your self…taking the necessary action to stop the cycle. Love is not conditional. To follow the Master, we must break the cycle with ourselves and with our children.

April 28
Father Would Have You Love

"Father simply loves you. And when you seem to fail your lessons, He does not stop loving you. He would *never* withhold His Perfect Love, not even for an instant. You will learn to love as He would have you love. This is by far the most difficult of all the lessons in our curriculum.

You cannot learn this lesson in one day, but you can begin by simply understanding and trusting Me in these words of great truth. Father loves you not because of what you say and do, but because of Who He is. He is Love, and Love is unconditional."

See your self...accepting the difficulty in this one lesson so often repeated. And it is not a lesson easily learned. More trust is necessary in these words of great truth. An unconditional Lover is Who our Father is. You have His genes.

April 29
Love Bears No Grudges

"Would you gain proficiency in unconditional love, My beloveds? Then you must forgive all. And you must learn to forgive and *forget*. Perhaps you have said, "I can forgive but I cannot forget." Forgetting is not easy.

Father fully understands it is not easy to forget much of the pain and suffering you have received from the unloving ministrations of conditional lovers. But when you fail to release *any* brother or sister from the captivity of your unforgiveness, you become the captive. Think on this."

See you self...taking the time this very day to find any unreleased prisoners from your "forgive and but can't forget" category. "Forgetting is not easy." The Teacher forgave His tormentors right from Calvery's cross. Think on this. You can forgive and forget or it would not be a part of our curriculum.

April 30
Repeat After Me

"Today we are repeating an earlier lesson. Why? All habituate conditional love! Thus an earlier lesson bears repeating. Repetition will, indeed, fortify our lessons. Day by day, I ask you to simply forgive *anyone* who has wronged you in any way. Put it out of your thinking. Bearing grievances day in and day out is counter-productive. It wastes our precious time.

Make a sincere effort to keep the gardens of your thinking weed free. Remember that each day is a beautiful gift. And when you labor to release *all* captives, it is a labor with great reward and so very worth your concentrated effort."

> *See your self*...accepting fully the lesson that bearing any grudges against any brother or sister is definitely counter-productive to your mental gardening. Every captive to disabling mental garbage must be set free. Bearing fruit is the reward and "very worth your concentrated effort."

MAY

May 1
Freely Have You Received

"I would teach you a simple precept.

Most of your grievances (or should I say grudges?) come simply from a lack of understanding. Seek to understand godly love. Love carries no burdens. Love bears no grudges. Love is free.

Early each morning take the few minutes necessary to loose any burden that you might carry. Follow in the footsteps of Father's Love. You can do this. I will *never* ask for more than you can give.

Give the gift of unconditional love, for freely you have received this gift."

See your self... taking the few minutes necessary early in your day to release all grievances and burdens. Why carry such nonsense as grievances and burdens into the precious and unconditionally loving gift of each new day? Why, indeed?

May 2
Take No Captives

"You have heard it said of old, My beloveds, that "I have come to set the captives free." That is truth. And the world today groans in the captivity of unforgiveness.

You *must* forgive. This is a necessary task, yes, a chore for each day. And one day you will be free from the only captivity there is. And it becomes an easy task to stay free.

You understand now the simple principle to bear no grudges. You will soon notice how it is possible to take no captives including yourself.

Isn't it far easier to simply say, "Let it go?" In truth, haven't you discovered the counter-productivity of grudge bearing? My beloveds, it simply isn't worth the effort."

See your self...accepting fully how very counter-productive grudge bearing actually is. Think of all the wasted moments mentally massacring the unaware captives to unforgiveness. Spare them all as well as your Self this very day.

May 3
Your Dark Clouds

"To bear one grudge against another brother or sister brings a dark cloud into our beautiful day. And one by one all the dark clouds will move away until there are only days of total sunshine.

And this truth remains; you are the reason for the cloudy days, My children. Anger and angst hide the Son-shine. However, the sun is always shinning above the clouds of your own negativity. You have made your own prisons, My Brothers and Sisters. These are mental prisons and I *will* lead you to freedom.

I will teach you the way to the heavenly kingdom. Day by day we go *together*. Simply listen and follow My words."

See your self...resisting *all* anger and angst against any Brother and Sister. Learn this lesson well and all mental dark clouds roll away. It is not an easy lesson for most of us but well worth the effort to try.

May 4
Let The Sun Shine

"Bring no negative thinking into today, beloveds. Is that not the best way to begin each day? Come to Me each morning to receive the lesson plan and come in total freedom from *any* negative thinking.

I have asked that you bear no grudges from the day before. Was there someone who made you angry yesterday? Set them free! There is no need to review the whys or wherefores of that anger. There is no need to think about the injustice, or remember that you were treated unfairly. Simply say, "I forgive."

And were you angry with yourself? Did you act unkindly toward another brother or sister? There is no need to castigate your self. Simply let it go. Cast the burden of negativity from your thinking. Then see the dark clouds roll away and the sun begin to shine."

*See your self...*accepting negativity as an unnecessary burden that indeed darkens the gift or each beautiful new day. Who needs such darkness? Surely not you!

May 5
Each Day Is A New Day

"Each day is a new day, a new beginning. Today lies before us and we have new territory to cover *together*. Let us take only love into today. Let us remember that we are here to spread our Father's Love to all we meet. Yes, let us *clothe* ourselves with kindness and gentle loving speech.

We go in His Love and His Light each and every day. Receive His gentle Touch of Love this morning. Let His Love light our Path and beckon us onward."

*See your self...*clothing your Self in His Love, as a gentle garment, you put on every day. Yes, *far more important* than the physical garments you clothe your Self with each day.

May 6
Words That Wound

"Your Father loves you, My beloveds. Let His Love propel you onward! You can project to all you meet a new gentleness, a new caring.

You can use your eyes to see what He would have you see and your ears to hear what He would have you hear. You can turn away from *all* that is dark and bring light to *every* place you set your foot.

Say 'no' to words that wound. The wounds of the tongue leave brutal scars, do they not? You know, for you have been wounded by words that caused grievous pain. And we will wound no one today. Turn away from *any* wounding through your words."

> *See your self...*in agreement to use your eyes and ears to see and hear *only* what our Father would have you see and hear. And step to a new mental height, by using your tongue to speak *only* what our Father would have you speak. Is this possible? Absolutely!

May 7
The Tongue Is A Tool

"This lesson is difficult, but you *must* begin to think carefully before you speak. Wound no one. This tool is a tool that can greatly advance the Kingdom of Heaven, but it can also set the Kingdom spiraling on a great backward path.

Indeed, Father can use your eyes and ears and tongue today. These tiny members *will* bring salvation to the world. And today you will begin to use these body members wisely.

Sow only love. Plant your gardens well. Fruit is always the goal in the heavenly kingdom within. The weeds must go, My Brothers and Sisters. *All* the weeds must go."

See your self...removing all the weeds of negative thinking. Sometimes in the natural weeds resemble flowers. Not so. Weeds are weeds in the natural and also in the mental area. Seek always for a mental weed-free environment.

May 8
Take His Love Into The World

"You will begin a new phase of our curriculum today, My beloved Brothers and Sisters. We are ready to take His Love into all of the world. We will take the gospel of Love wherever we go. Impact the little world that surrounds you now. Cast your love abroad. Cast your love like seeds, to multiply and replenish the earth."

See your self...in the Father's Business. His Business is replenishing His earth with Love. And you will find your Self gainfully employed as you sow His "Love Product" today.

May 9
Pearls Of Great Price

"Our Father has placed His Seal of Love on all that lives and breathes and moves. And in you resides the potential for His greatest Accomplishments to all His Creation. You are all pearls in His Sight. You are all pearls of very great price, even beyond your knowing.

Let us think today on this pearl of great price. Love is that pearl. Love begins as a tiny seed. You know of the planting in the womb of the tiny, miniscule seed that is life. And yes, love is life and life is love. All life is love, a pearl of infinite value.

You find it difficult to place so great a price upon your worth, but Father does not. For now, simply trust Me that this is truth. He has created you in love, to be love. You are but a seed pearl in the great adventure. And the sands of time will bring you to fruition; of this you can be very sure."

*See your self...*now as the seed pearl, created in love to become Love. Trust this truth and daily grow toward fruition.

May 10
Irritants Of Life

"Yes the irritants of life create your luster. Oh, you will shine one day, My Beloveds, but first the lessons. The lessons are the Path to great beauty and you are on that Path. Step out firmly today. There is nothing to fear, for I go with you and I am delighted with every step you take.

Father delights in your progress on the Path. Your daily kindness and gentle loving concern for one another do not go unnoticed. He knows your every struggle and applauds your every victory."

*See your self...*accepting the daily irritants as creating a marvelous luster on your own little pearl. And try to understand that all your lessons with Father's Help and His amazing Love, are creating a pearl of great price.

May 11
Find More Joy

"Find more joy in each day, My children, for indeed, you do progress in many ways beyond your understanding.

You are too hard on yourselves! You ponder your supposed failures and you grow discouraged far too easily.

Have I reminded you that each day is a beautiful gift? Have I not called you to thanksgiving for the gift of life? Yes, there is much to be thankful for in *every* day. And I ask you today to count your blessings.

Remove your thinking from the one or two things in your day that are not positive. You will find that in retrospect the positive far outweighs the negative with a simple change in attitude."

See your self...examining your attitude. Does it need a change from negative to positive? Do it!

May 12
You Are The Captain

"You are the captain of your attitude. You can make a simple change in the direction of the entire day by refusing to harbor *any* negative thoughts.

Yes, this day is a beautiful gift. Be thankful, most thankful, for the power and the freedom to run and reign supreme over your thought life. You are improving, and you do indeed, bring our Father great delight with every advance in this area. We are very pleased with your growth."

See your self...with power and freedom in the area of your thought life. Salute the captain you actually are and venture forward into the marvelous gift of today with positive steps in the direction to continually delight our Father by your positive thought choices.

May 13
How Does Your Garden Grow?

"We do advance, My Brothers and Sisters. Think how short a period of time has passed since we began this journey to remove the negative weeds from the garden of your thought life.

With every passing day our garden tasks grow easier. Our gardens grow more beautiful and the sunshine in our days far outweighs the scattered dark clouds of negativity.

If you have some weeding to do today in your thought life, do it now! Pause a moment. Say no to any dark thoughts before we take each other's hand and begin the day. No need to carry any unnecessary baggage. And should the negative return, simply say no.

And so we together have set about the happy task of casting seeds of love in our gardens, and yes, also daily sowing a liberal sprinkling of kindness and merciful acts."

> *See your self...*early in this day, taking a few minutes to remove any weedy thinking from your thought life. Then follow closely the wise suggestion to liberally sprinkle kind and merciful acts throughout the gift of this day already filled with the sunshine of your beautiful thoughts.

May 14
Seeds Of Love

"You are careful gardeners now. Each morning you remove any negative thinking. You have made forgiveness a daily habit. No longer do you carry the heavy burden of unforgiveness.

We set about each day to forgive one another as He forgives. We follow in His Footsteps and we have discovered that His loving and merciful Path leads to peace and yes, to great happiness.

Again I say to be sure you walk the Path today in total love. Do whatever is necessary to walk in freedom."

> *See your self...*accepting the Love Path as the walkway to great freedom. Walk in His Footsteps and daily see your personal growth in happiness.

May 15
In The Service Of Love

"Love is the Path to freedom. You have come far, My Beloveds, but Indeed, we have far to go. Love one another. Forgive all. Carry no grudges.

You have been commissioned in the service of Love. It is an honor to serve our Father's Will. He wants you to freely spread His Gospel of Love to every soul throughout the world.

He calls you each day to this service. Be kind. Be gentle. Be ministers of mercy. This is not always easy, My children. But *every* effort in His Service brings great delight to all who watch your progress."

See your self ... enlisted in the Service to our Father's Will. And no kindness, no merciful or gentle loving act is overlooked or forgotten by those who watch us from the unseen dimension.

May 16
A Heavenly Host

"A heavenly host surround you with great love, and yes, devotion. You are not lonely ministers of His Love. You are surrounded on every side by a great host of heavenly watchers and caretakers.

And in truth, they delight in all your efforts as do I. They are here to help you clear away the weeds and prepare the soil for the Paradise of His Intent.

Indeed, we are all in service to His Will.

Keep going! You do well, and you will continue to do well, of that you can be very sure, for I AM with you."

See your self ...in the company of the heavenly host as well as the great I AM. You are not alone. And you do well, for I AM assures you of this and He travels with you every step of the way.

May 17
We Walk In His Love

"This is a new day, My children. You delight our Father so very much. He knows the Path you tread is not always easy. He sees you struggle with difficulties. He knows you have been hurt, and so often you have all felt the arrows of rejection. And every arrow has left a scar. Yet He offers a healing balm today for every pain and sorrow.

Release all those who have sent the arrows of searing pain and you will see even the scars disappear. It only takes a minute to attain freedom, to walk renewed in His Love."

See your self...walking in freedom by releasing any one who has hurt you. Release the unforgiven captives and walk on leaving all those nasty scars behind, even those that were self-inflicted.

May 18
A Daily Inventory

"I will ask you often in the days ahead to renew the pledge of forgiveness. Yes, I said pledge. Will you not this very day, make a vow of the heart to hold no one captive to unforgiveness? For Indeed, it is far easier to walk the path in love than the alternative.

Each day, take a quick inventory of the garden of your thought life. Today is our Father's gift and we can bless all those who share the gift with us by sharing His Love with all.

Examine your thoughts for the weeds of unforgiveness. Simply remove them, leaving space in the garden for seeds of love to grow."

See your self...renewing the pledge of forgiveness. Release all captives and attempt to take no more. See unforgiveness as the great weed it is and how it hampers the growth of freedom in our thinking.

May 19
The Fruit Of Love

"My beloved children let us walk the Path of Love. Little kindnesses and gentle words are the seeds we cast upon our Path today. And there in the sunshine of these loving acts, the fruit of love will bloom. Soon our gardens will be full to overflowing with ever-blooming fruit.

This seems impossible in the darkness of the cloudy days, but faith draws us forward. Our faith is the hope that love will bloom when there is no evidence. I tell you the truth. Cast the seeds and you will see the return."

*See your self...*accepting by faith that you *will* see fruit for every seed of love you cast about today and for every seeding you perform in all the days ahead.

May 20
Your Seeds Will Bear Fruit

"You have said oft times, "How can I love when there is no return?" But we take a new gospel. We take the gospel of forgiveness. And I tell you now in this moment, these seeds of love you sow will bear fruit. And you will see an abundant harvest.

With the weeding chores behind us, we step happily forward, knowing we go in our Father's Will. We will walk the Path in His Love today.

Keep Sowing! You will reap, My children, and it will be a harvest beyond your imagination. Our Father delights in your daily garden labors. Indeed, He has chosen well the Ambassadors of His Will."

See your self...as a chosen one, and one who truly delights our Father with your daily efforts to walk in His Will and His Ways.

May 21
Love Is Our Labor

"As the month progresses, let Me remind you, My beloved children, of our Father's daily Business, with always new seeds to sow and yes, more fruit to harvest.

I tell you the truth. You do well, My children. Again I say you are far too hard on yourselves, and yes, you are far too hard on your brothers and sisters. Your expectations are too high and you grow impatient with your progress.

There is no hurry. The Path will present the curriculum necessary for the progress of our Father's expectations. Put your expectations aside. The Plan is Perfect, for you as well as for your brothers and sisters. Each day is sufficient for itself."

See your self...finally accepting the perfection of our Father's Plan. How could it be any other way except absolutely perfect? Oh, if only we would remember P.P. (Perfect Plan) in all our trials and tribulations.

May 22
Wherever You Go

"I have presented to you a plan for each of our days. A little review now and then will set us perfectly on the Path. Begin each day in the forgiveness mode. Release all anger and angst. Clear your Path in the gift of each day.

Enter the day with gentle, kind and merciful thoughts. Enter the day with the vow to love all you meet upon the Path. Smile often. Remember the love of God you are gifted with and take this love forward wherever you go.

You are the inheritors of His Legacy. His Will is that you love one another. You need not seek His Will; it has found you."

See your self...having inherited His divine Loving Nature, as simply passing it forward. Love is His Gift that keeps on giving.

May 23
Overflowing Hearts

"You must fill your hearts to overflowing and take His abundant Love to all the world. I send you forward into your own little worlds each day. And at the end of your day count the blessings you have received. Did you smile often today? Did you hug a brother or sister and let them know they are children beloved of God?

This is an easy Path we tread when you sow God's Perfect Love. If you are willing to sow, He will present you with many opportunities to serve His Will on earth.

Be happy! The service of Love is our labor and its profits are abundant beyond anything you can imagine.

Take My hand in yours and together we will lighten the burdens for all we meet upon the Path today with the blessed generosity of our happy attitude."

See you self...giving the love you have so freely received. Your happiness is an acknowledgment of Whose child you are and how happily His Love has infected your attitude.

May 24
Lower Your Expectations

"Disappointment is birthed in too high expectations. I have told you that you expect far too much of yourself and each other. And of course, parents expect far too much of their children. This is where the false idea is birthed of God's high expectations. And from this erroneous belief, the weeds of disappointment and depression are planted.

How many times you have been disappointed! Why? You wanted something you didn't get, and then you became depressed. What is depression then? Nothing more than a temper tantrum! Depression is refusing to function because you cannot have your own way in life.

These words may seem harsh, but they are truth. There are many that have suffered great disappointments, and indeed great depressing moods, and they can descend upon you like the blackest clouds, obscuring all the sunshine. But I say to you today, a mood is a mood."

> *See your self*...releasing all the high expectations you have
> falsely planted upon your brothers and sisters, as well as so
> often planted upon your Self. Accept, allow and surrender
> to the fact that life presents disappointments and you
> cannot have your own way in every situation.

May 25
Master Your Moods

"Look about you this day. Some are happy! Some are not. I have told you to choose happiness. I have asked you to remove all negativity. Would I ask you to remove depression if it were something more than a mood? Of course not! Now I ask you to be kind to your Self.

We are learning some difficult lessons now, in this particular curriculum. Again, I am asking you to weed the garden of your thought life. And I am asking you to learn this lesson now. Depression is nothing more then a bad mood. And you can control your moods. You already know that is truth. But you live in a world with brothers and sisters who cannot control their moods. Therein lies the labor of our ministry.

You are in charge of your attitude. And life, the good life, is all about attitude, the attitude of a child of faith. If you trust the Father completely, as you profess, then a happy attitude is the garment that you put on each day."

See your self...clothed in the garment of a happy attitude.
Why choose any weedy garments? Why, indeed! Follow
the Master's great advice and master your attitude.

May 26
Ambassadors Of His Will

"You are the Ambassadors of our Father's Will on earth, My beloved children. I have asked you to plant the seeds of love, and to remove the weeds of anger and unforgiveness.

Today I ask you for a new growth experience. I am asking you to grow to a new maturity, and we will go deeply into the garden area of our thoughts. Indeed, the curriculum intensifies. You will attempt to choose happiness even in the great difficulties of life.

You have heard Me tell you that our Father's Will is perfect. His Plan for your life is perfect also, of that you can be very sure.

You rise each morning to the gift of each beautiful new day. You pull the weeds and you plant the seeds and you are now fully commissioned to take His Love into all the world.

There are multitudes that sow the seeds of love. You are not alone. Simply continue. You will see fruit. You do not labor in vain."

See your self...as truly fully commissioned in this amazing
work force sowing the Father's Love throughout His world.
He has chosen you wisely. He knows how very much love
you are capable of spreading. Continue onward. His Love
is the perfection that all mankind is seeking.

May 27
Officers Of His Peace

"Now let us dress ourselves as His Ambassadors. Let us look the part, as His Officers of Peace. Clothe yourselves in the uniform of His Service. A smile, a gentle word, a loving touch and the happy attitude of faith, these are the garments that you wear each day.

Simply think about these words. Meditate on how to clothe yourselves each day. If you need an attitude adjustment before you leave your prayer closet each morning, then simply do it.

Yes, I am teaching you a new way to pray and a new way to adorn yourselves for your labor in His Love. Read these words again before you step into this day. Meditate on the uniform of His Will."

*See your self...*following these very wise directives. And yes, as directed, read these words again. Make no mistake on the proper attire for the labor required in every workday. We labor in Love and receive the guaranteed reward of the peace that passes all understanding. One day you will hear these amazing words, "Well done, thou good and faithful servant."

May 28
Cultivate Good Cheer

"Be Happy! Smile often! Father is working *always* on your behalf. Be of good cheer! The Path gets easier to tread. You are growing beautifully and yes; you are gaining strength for the tasks of each day. In our gardens there are less weeds, and the seeds of love are growing fat. They are soon to produce the fruit you each long for so very much.

The tender care you give these personal little gardens will one day turn the whole Universe into the paradise of His Intent."

*See your self...*happy, cheerful and smiling often and of course, tenderly caring for your thought gardens. We are all by this careful garden tending, turning our world into the "paradise" of Father's perfect intention.

May 29
No Effort Too Small

"I know that often you feel that your feeble attempts do little in the scheme of universe enrichment, but I tell you now, there are no little acts of love. Love is a tremendous action. Love *is* changing the world constantly for the better.

Your little world is improving, is it not? Since you began the weeding and seeding process, isn't your own personal world a far happier place to dwell? Of course it is! We will take inventory often in how you progress.

And I say to you today, you do very well indeed. You are progressing beautifully. Your seeds of love will produce abundant fruit one day in a very weed-free garden. Together our harvest will feed the hungry."

*See your self...*changing the world, one person at a time. And yes, see your own personal world a far happier dwelling place for all your daily efforts to seed and weed.

May 30
His Love Gives Us Strength

"Step-by-step we go. We arise each day confident in Our Father's Love. The presence of His Love gives us all the strength we need to face the challenges of each day.

You see abundant fruit in your lives. You clothe yourselves daily in the garment of love. You gain proficiency now, in tender words and gentle touches. You are surprised often by a new excitement in your days. You are less fearful.

Now I ask you not to vacillate from the curriculum. You need to affirm to yourselves often that you are doing well. You are progressing beautifully. Work with Me. We shall prevail. His Will *will* be done."

*See your self...*happily accepting His Words of great encouragement. "You are progressing beautifully." And as He suggests affirm your Self often that you are doing well.

May 31
The Paradise Of His Intent

"Each day there are some stray weeds to remove. But you are getting better at spotting the weeds before they develop deep roots. You know that all bitterness and anger simply spoil the beauty of all that you wish to create.

Step-by-step, weed by weed, seed by seed, and yes, garden by garden, *we will create* the Paradise of His Intent.

Keep the words "The Paradise of His Intent" in your thought life, Meditate on that phrase often and then simply do your part to bring Father's Intent to reality. It is the consummate flower."

*See your self...*recognizing the part you personally play in the Creator's great script to make our very own world a "paradise." Scripture starts out "in the beginning" with the Paradise garden experience. How can we not recognize our Father's Intent and do all that we can to bring His Intent to fruition?

JUNE

June 1
Reap What You Sow

"Yes, My beloved children, 'the Paradise of His Intent' will come, and in certain aspects it has come already, for *you* are creating your own little Paradise on Earth where you happily labor.

Paradise was never intended as a work-free environment.

You will *always* have the daily chores of pulling weeds and planting seed, for clearly there will never be a harvest without the preparation of the soil for sowing, and then the planting of the seed and then the gathering of the harvest.

Life is *always* sowing and reaping, My children. And without a doubt you most certainly reap what you sow."

> *See your self*...accepting fully the daily chore of pulling all the weeds from your mental gardens. And also daily sowing gentle, kind, loving and merciful acts, as is the Father's Intention for all His children. You have your Father's genes. You can follow His Intention to sow and reap according to His Perfect Plan.

June 2
Days Of Our Lives

"The weeds of anger, bitterness and discontent spoil the garden and they definitely take up valuable space where the very beautiful flowers of love could blossom.

Love is our Father's Will for all His Universes. You will toil all the days of your lives in His Will to love one another. So be content to understand the Plan. You are here in this earth experience to sow and to reap. You will sow love and you will reap love. That is the Father's Intent for all His Children. You will labor in His Will."

*See your self...*in total acceptance now of this Perfect Plan. Yes, accept, allow and surrender to the Father's Perfect Will.

June 3
The Long Haul

"Look about your gardens today. Think about the chores that need performing. Are there a few weeds to pull perhaps? Just do it! And much love to sow? Of course!

You are getting acclimated to the terrain we tread *together*. Loving one another is becoming less of a chore and more of a habit, isn't it? And you are beginning to settle in for the long haul.

Love is a joyous habit. Love is a beautiful garment in which to clothe yourselves each day."

*See your self...*pulling any weeds that need pulling today. And then dressing your Self in this heavenly garment as suggested by our Teacher and Friend Who definitely shares this Path we walk together each day.

June 4
Walk In His Image

"My beloved children, loving one another is the only true responsibility for the Ambassadors of our Father's Will. And we are learning to love. Love starts with the merciful act of forgiveness.

It has been said "to forgive is divine." Total forgiveness is the Father's character. He holds no one accountable for their past. And yes, I said *no one*.

This is very hard to understand because you have been raised from the cradle to believe in crime and punishment. And you believe that this teaching has come as a mandate from our Father. But I tell you Love forgives.

And that is truth. Love is unconditional forgiveness. If you truly understood this, all further need for learning would cease."

> *See your self*...forgiving your Self for all your failures in the unconditional love category. And begin today to try with all your heart and soul to learn to love as our Father loves, and as He would have you love.

June 5
Unconditional Forgiveness

"There is so much in this difficult teaching that I would say to you today, but let it suffice that we go hand in hand each day through this learning experience.

Be content to take all the steps necessary without hurry; and yes without fear. You *will* walk in the Father's Love and you *will* learn to unconditionally forgive. For to walk in His Image, you must walk in His Character."

> *See your self*...relaxing into a "no hurry" and "no worry" mode of walking each day. Our Father is in no particular rush for you to walk in His Character and why should we rush through the lessons? A degree in patience is clearly the fruit from this love curriculum.

June 6
Father Understands

"Would you represent our Father well in this life experience? Then simply love one another.

This is a growing process. Maturity comes slowly, My children. There is a saying, "two steps forward and one step back is still moving forward." Ah, but you give yourselves little credit for the forward steps and suffer greatly for the *seeming* backward movement.

Father looks upon His Children with great delight in every forward action. And what of the seeming backward step? Every child must take some tumbles along the Path. That is how the toddler learns to walk, is it not?

Release the burden of your seeming failures. Father understands the tumbles. He is not given nearly enough credit for the beauty of His Depth of Understanding. He appreciates ever so much the countless times you have stumbled, only to rise again and continue on."

> *See your self...* releasing the burden of your seeming failures. You are surprised to learn today of the magnificent understanding of our Parent from on High. His understanding far excels all others.

June 7
The Gardening Process

"Again today, let us consider the gardening process. You are growing beautifully, and one day you will blossom continuously in "the Paradise of His Intent."

I choose to remind you again today of His Intention. It is truly a garden of ever-blooming Love. Many of you have done gardening in your life experience. Where, oh where, do all the weeds come from? They are constantly appearing and the garden needs constant attention. Yes, and it is ever the same with the gardens of our minds."

See your self...in need of this reminder today, for we all
do tend to forget the appointed Path. Loving one another
is the appointed Path and the blossoms from the Love Path
will turn our earth experience into a very grand Paradise,
Indeed.

June 8
Our Daily Garden

"Our gardens require constant weeding, do they not, My children? You must
be diligent to remove every weed. You must remind yourself persistently
that the weeds can easily overrun the garden and crowd out the potential for
the blossoms ever to appear. So we diligently remove every weed every day.

Today is no different than any other. Remove the weeds early in the
day. Forgive all that have offended you and be careful today that you cast
no weeds in a brother or sister's garden. Keep your own garden weed free,
and cause no brother or sister the extra pain of weeding their own garden
from your intent."

See your self...casting no seeds of mental weeds today in
any brother or sister's garden, and certainly keep your own
garden weed free as well.

June 9
Guard Your Tongue

"Guard the doorway to your mind and place a serious guard upon your
tongue. The tongue, My children, is a very interesting member of the body.
It can be quite unruly; and for sure, you have never considered the amount
of weeds that are sown with this tiny member.

If you must weed from your own garden all the hurts and painful attacks
that have entered into your own thought process from other tongues, then

you most certainly must consider all the weeds you have caused to grow in your brothers' and sisters' gardens.

You must be careful, for while many beautiful seeds are sown with the tongue, many weeds are cast about with the same instrument."

> *See your self...*taking the necessary time to sow words of beauty and love, kindness and mercy into these gardens that surround your own. Words can both attack and lift up. You are commissioned to love and you will answer that very worthy commission from above.

June 10
Truth Is A Pruning Implement

"Truth is a sharp pruning implement. Truth attacks the weeds with great diligence.

I have said that all of this life experience is sowing and reaping. I remind you again that what you sow, you reap. If you sow weeds you reap weeds. And we are concerned today with the weeds you cast about with the tongue.

This is not a lesson you learn in one day. The habits of weed sowing are very deeply embedded in your thought systems. But you will receive all the help you need, for in truth, you are learning quickly now."

> *See your self...*gladly accepting that you *will* receive all the help you need in learning to put a guard on your tongue and to think before you speak. Sowing weeds is surely not your daily intention.

June 11
Our Father's Intention

"And so, My beloved children, with the simple truth that the tongue casts weeds as well as seeds of great beauty, we begin a deeper lesson Plan.

You are responsible for your own garden's planting and weeding. But you also must refrain from planting weeds in another's garden. And equally important is it for you to understand that you can plant fruitful seeds in all the gardens that surround you. You will begin to "see" now with the vision of our Father's Intention.

How does this universe become the "Paradise of His Intent?" Ah, with weeding and seeding, in both your own gardens and your brothers' and sisters'. The Brotherhood that is Father's Intent increases garden by garden. And today you "see" the vision, do you not?

Oh, we will become very busy gardeners in the days and weeks ahead. I did tell you this would be a very interesting month."

> *See you self...*working in our Father's Business. Yes, of course, you are employed in the Family Business and thus are delighted to work towards something so wonderful as bringing Paradise to earth.

June 12
Fertilize Your Soil

"I have asked you, My children, to begin each day by erasing all the weeds of unforgiveness. Forgiveness is mercy. You do not always immediately understand the lessons, but faith grows one step at a time.

Trust blooms in your garden when faith is patiently exercised. Simply listen each day to the lessons and try to practice them as best you know how.

All of these are connected, mercy, kindness, forgiveness, trust, faith, goodness and love. These are the fertilizers for your garden that help to create "the Paradise of His Intent.""

With the understanding of our Father's Intent, we can simply go about the Father's Business, creating beauty and abundance."

See your self...actively employed in the family business and doing all that is required in this amazing employment. Be sincerely delighted to have found your place in His Perfect Plan.

June 13
Think Before Speaking

"You stumble occasionally. You have difficulty with anger, perhaps. But you are beginning to master that little weed that truly spoils our garden. You see more clearly now that many of the stings and arrows, the little slights and injustices that you have endured along life's path, have come for the most part from a lack of understanding. And equally so, you yourselves have planted some painful weeds.

Now we begin the practice of thinking before we speak. We no longer desire to litter the gardens that surround us.

Yes, My children, it is in these gardens, the gardens of your thinking, that we must diligently labor each day."

See your self...as one, perhaps, who so often lashed out in anger, with little thought to the pain you may have inflicted. How wise is the admonition from our Teacher today, to "think before speaking." How very wise, indeed!

June 14
Sow The Seeds Of Love

"We go each day to sow Love. The gardens are beginning to bloom. And when there is no apparent evidence yet of Love's bloom, we continue in faith to sow, as He would have us sow. And our faith grows.

We sow because we know it is His Will. We sow because we do not doubt that the fruit of our labors *will* bloom. Yes, My dear ones, the promise of fruit is real. Sowing and reaping is the way of this Path's intention."

See your self...exercising your Faith, fully believing that sowing love will reap fruit. There is no room for *any* doubt whatsoever in this very great truth.

June 15
Self Will Must Die

"There is no doubt now that the lessons are taking root in the gardens of your thought life.

Always there are the weeds of negativity to persistently remove. And always there are the seeds of love to unfailingly sow. And again and again, I will remind you that you do well, My Brothers and Sisters, in both the weeding and the sowing.

I know this Path is not easy. Often you have walked this Path in self-will, with a lack of regard for our Father's Will. You have cast the weeds of discontent and animosity with little thought for the feelings of others. Now the understanding has come that self-will must die."

See your self...with a new awareness, that self-will is not our Father's Will, nor could it ever be His Will for His children. Let us begin this very day to totally seek Heaven's Will for Father's Kingdom on earth."

June 16
Prune Your Memories

"It is a beautiful new day. Are there any of your brothers and sisters that you hold captive today? Is there anyone you need to forgive? And what of yourselves? Take a few moments to review. Think about a few moments in your yesterday when perhaps a negative mood descended like a dark cloud.

You need to release yourselves from those little negative moments. And release, as well, any of your brothers and sisters that you hold captive today in your negative thoughts. Simply say, "I forgive." And if you find your thoughts returning today to *any* negative happenstance, you may refuse that thought immediately.

Scatter all dark clouds away."

*See your self...*walking in the gift of this beautiful new day totally in the Son-shine. If He tells us to leave the dark clouds of all our yesterday's behind us, then do it! These instructions are incredibly clear and there is no need for any misunderstanding.

June 17
The Power Of Choice

"Through God's gift of free will, the power of choice is always yours. In this moment you can choose freedom. And you are free to choose the good thoughts. Keep the sun shining in God's Will, all day long. Grow in the knowledge that you are the captain of your thinking. And you can be free with a simple "no" to negativity.

All your thoughts, each and every one of the thoughts you think, are, indeed, a personal choice. Choose your thoughts well, My children, as you choose what seeds to grow in your garden."

*See your self...*choosing every thought now with great discernment. Understand fully the power of choice is a completely free will choice. Your mind is a beautiful place and how you choose to decorate it belongs completely to you. Choose wisely.

June 18
Center Your Thinking

"Good Morning, My children. I will again today speak to you on the power of choice. You can choose where you center your thinking. Now we begin a very real advance in your Path to freedom when you learn to center your mind on good will.

Release all the deep-seated bad habits of long standing. You need not be the victim of your negative thinking. Choose sunshine and resist the dark clouds.

Resist the dark clouds of negativity and they will flee, like the fog flees from the sunshine on a fog-bound day."

*See your self...*resisting all the dark clouds of negativity. You will no longer be the victim of negative thinking. This is a new day where you are determined to stay in the now and in the sunshine of your happy attitude.

June 19
The Willful Choice

"You spend these few minutes each morning centering on the will of our Father. I have told you of His Delight in your happiness. And I again bring your attention to the truth that you can bring our Father delight over and over again by your willful choice to love.

Seek His Will *always,* for therein lies your happiness. When you love one another, He is delighted. When you begin your days with our Father's Will for merciful forgiveness as your will for your day, then know full well that in truth, you are a delight to Him.

Remember always, there is no other way to peace than walking in our Father's Will. We walk this Path *together* in His Will."

See your self...totally in alignment with the Perfect Will of our heavenly Father, and in this willful alignment you do bring Him great delight.

June 20
Keys To The Kingdom

"You have each been given the Keys to the Kingdom of Heaven on Earth. These keys are the simple rules that guide our way and guard our peace and happiness. There is no need to seek and search any further.

Love one another. Forgive each other's every offense. And walk the Path in truth. Follow the simple Path of Love. The Eternal Path stretches before us. You have found the Way and we walk together hand in hand in an ever upward ascent."

See your self...ascending a proverbial Stairway to Paradise here in Father's earthly Kingdom. And hand and hand with our Teacher and our Friend like no other, you know you will make it to the top of that ever-ascending stairway.

June 21
Homeward Bound

"Yes, I take your hand each day, My beloved children. You are never alone.

Each day we climb higher in our ascent toward our heavenly home. We are ever homeward bound. But I have said before that our journey entails the accomplishment of Our Father's Will on the earthly plain. And you are His Choices as Ambassadors of His Will.

As you learn, you teach. You teach by example. You are here to sow Love and to reap always the harvest of what you sow. Each day is a new beginning."

> *See your self...*climbing ever higher, always homeward bound. And while we labor for His Kingdom, sowing and reaping bountifully in His Love labor, we know we do labor in His Will. That is a labor so satisfying and most gratifying.

June 22
His Army Of Officers

"I have asked you to clothe yourselves in a uniform that is easily recognized as one in His Army of Officers. You need to review these little rules for officer's training. A smile, a gentle, loving touch and a kind word here and there, these are the garments of love.

Be sure to dress yourselves early each day as you walk forward into His Will and His Way for your day. Clothe yourselves in the sunshine of a happy face.

You know He loves you unconditionally. And He sends you as unconditional lovers into a hungry and love-starved world. He has chosen well, His Ambassadors of Love.

You do make a difference!"

> *See your self...*dressing for the part you play each day in His Will and His Way. Let there remain no doubt in anyone's mind, Whose Army you serve in and Who is, indeed, your Commanding Officer.

June 23
Children Of God

"I will remind you often of who you are and Whom you serve, and you will never grow tired of these reminders.

Yes, remember always, Whose children you are, beloveds. You are the Children of God, thus you are *all* Brothers and Sisters in His Family. Therein is a tremendous Unity of Spirit, where there is no separation. Love will bring the unity of the Father's Will to this world. It is a step-by-step transformation that we undertake together."

See your self...as the most beloved child of God; daily seeking His Will, never in a hurry and serving happily for as long as it takes for this world's much longed for transformation.

June 24
We Are His Garden

"We pull the weeds of anger, animosity and discontent each day from the gardens of our thinking. Step-by-step we remove and release every brother and sister held captive in unforgiveness. Daily we sow love. And we know that it is easier to sow Love in a soil free of weeds.

Take the time to labor in His Will each day. His Will is no longer a mystery. And you understand fully now the need for the daily maintenance of your gardens. If you desire the fruits from Love, you must first pull all the weeds and plant the seeds that will produce the fruit. And you are the keeper of your brother's garden, as well as your own."

See your self...actively involved in these daily gardening chores. The Father's Will is your will and you will take the time this very day to sow some love seed's in a brother or sister's garden as well as your own.

June 25
His Kingdom Come

"Today another beautiful dawn is gifted to us. We have many opportunities to further God's Kingdom. We will not turn our backs on the labor necessary. We are here to sow freely our Father's Love. And we will not disappoint Him. He has chosen well.

Yes, we desire to sow for a mighty harvest. His Kingdom comes slowly, as some of you perceive. But take all these forward steps now, My Brothers and Sisters, with total assurance that His Kingdom *will* come. Of that you need never doubt."

> *See your self...* free from all doubt that His Kingdom will come, and His Will *will* be done on earth, in Answer to that mighty prayer that countless have offered through all the centuries. Indeed, His Will *will* not fail to be mightily evidenced.

June 26
Peace Is The Fruit Of Our Labor

"We advance slowly but surely, My Beloved children. The Kingdom of Our Father's Will is ever our goal. We will never lose sight of His eternal Will that we love one another.

Many have sown seeds of hatred, and the fruit of their ill-fated sowing has been war and destruction. But we sow only seeds of love now and peace is the fruit of our labor."

> *See your self...* always working in this gardening atmosphere; ever sowing love and reaping peace. What other will but His is your choice for this life experience when the guarantee of peace for your labor is the reward for service to His Will? No other will but His is our choice.

June 27
Crowd Of Witnesses

"As you diligently labor, do not think that your little daily efforts pass unnoticed. You do impact the little worlds that surround each and every one of you.

You are surrounded on every side by a great crowd of witnesses. Paul, My Servant, told you this so many centuries ago.

Many have waited through the centuries to see the dawning of this generation. You will be remembered as the children who heard this message of great truth and took this message as directed into all of the world.

The gospel of forgiveness goes forth now in strength never before witnessed. And you will reap a mighty harvest for Our Father's Glory, My beloveds. You *will* reap as no other generation has ever reaped before. The Kingdom of His Intent is here, and all in the heavens rejoice at its coming."

See your self... greatly impacting His world with His Love for all His children. His Grace allows *every* child ever birthed entrance into His ever-expanding family. It is His Intent for all His children to find their place in His Kingdom.

June 28
Rules Of Service

"My beloved children let us review the rules of service.

You have been instructed to put on the garments of Love. A smile is an easy uniform to wear when all goes well. And giving the gift of a gentle touch and a kind word are easy tasks to perform. But I must remind you of My Words from long ago. "Whatsoever you do to the least of one of these you do it for Me." Such service will require that you love one another as I do, unconditionally.

Invite every brother and sister into the warmth of My unconditional love."

See your self... happily embracing the role of our Master's intention as an unconditional lover of all that share your Path today. Is this possible? Of course, or it would not be His suggestion for each and every one of our Father's children.

June 29
Unconditional Forgiveness

"Think today of the one that is not welcome in your home. Think of the one you cannot forgive. Is there someone you have shut a door to and forbidden entrance into you heart?

I ask you now to allow that forbidden person back into your heart. Search your thinking well this morning My children. Go down the pathway of your memory and release again any brother or sister held captive to your unforgiveness.

Be very sure that no one is standing outside in the cold of your merciless unforgiveness."

See your self... graciously forgiving every offense and releasing the hurts and wounds of your life experience. Be merciful to all that share your Path, for that is our Father's Will for all His children.

June 30
The Gift Of Love

"There is no greater Gift of Love than unconditional forgiveness. You have this gift freely given to you each day. Do not be fearful to give it away to all who have need of it.

Father bestows His Gift of Love on you in an abundant, never ending supply. Give as you have received.

This Gift of Love is yours to give, just as it has been given to you moment by moment. There has *never* been a moment in your whole existence when you have been removed from our Father's Love, nor will there ever be such a moment.

You do not move in and out of His Love. It is as constant as the rising of the sun."

See your self... with greater consistency in the extension of this Perfect Gift. Love, so freely given is yours to share with all who share our Path each day.

JULY

July 1
Love With Consistency

"You must love with consistency. You are called to love one another and you will answer that call. You will answer that call today and every day in His Service. You will step forward each day into the gift of each day with love in your hearts.

You are a small army of Lovers, but you will grow. The seeds you plant each day *will* blossom and bear fruit.

Give no thought for tomorrow. Fill your hearts in this very moment with all the love seeds sufficient for today. Garb yourselves in gentleness and kindness and prepare to return the gift of this day to Him Who is the Source of all Love."

See your self... loving with consistency. Every love seed you plant *will* blossom and bear fruit. Love is always fruitful. It's a heavenly guarantee.

July 2
Trust Father's Plan

"I ask you this morning, My beloved children, to trust completely in our Father's Plan for the salvation of His Universe. Return our Father's great gift with every fiber of your being. Cast your love freely, and prepare for the abundant return.

You will not sow in vain, My Brothers and Sisters. There is never one seed of love that falls from a loving heart without a return thereof. Remember always, the seeds of love *never fail* to produce blossoms."

> *See your self*...trusting completely in our Father's Perfect Plan. In all its perfection, loving one another will *always* produce a bountiful harvest.

July 3
Mercy-Filled Words

"We spend these few minutes together each morning to prepare ourselves mentally for the day.

We release everyone who has harmed us with hurtful words or the slights of rejection.

We simply say these mercy-filled words, "I forgive" and in so doing we release all the captives we have held in the merciless bonds of unforgiveness.

We take a few minutes to clothe ourselves in the garments of our Father's Love.

We prepare to venture forth, ready to love all we meet. And then we advance, unafraid, yes, with courage, for whatever mystery this day holds.

Refuse no brother or sister the joy and happiness they will receive when you extend His Love to each and every one that you meet along the path of this beautiful day.

Be prepared to extend His loving Mercy freely to all."

> *See your self*...clothed in the garments of His Love. And as you leave this morning's meeting with the One Who councils so wisely, do all that you have been so wisely instructed to do. Be a doer of His Word, not just a hearer.

July 4
Independent Spirit

"The Father loves you all. There are no conditions to His Love. And if you have received a conditional gospel, it is false. You are asked to live in this truth.

The Father loves *all* His children, of every nation and every tribe. You are *all* brothers and sisters, one family, one flesh. Go now in His Love each day to extend His boundless Love to all the Family, His and yours, for they are one and the same.

Show your independence from all that would hold you back from being His earnest Ambassador. Step forward without fear, in complete dependence on the Father, Who *will* provide your every need."

*See your self...*happily accepting this great promise that *every* need will be provided. Do you need to learn to walk more courageously in unconditional love for every brother and sister, from every nation and every tribe? Then relax. Yes, rest assured as that need *will* be supplied as needed.

July 5
The Golden Rule

"Love one another. That is Father's Plan for each of our days. The Golden Rule encompasses all of humanity. Do unto others as I would do unto you. I would love you and forgive you, as you will do unto others as well.

There is *nothing* in the Path of this day that we cannot face together. And we do go hand in hand; ready to serve our Father's children with all our love. Freely you have received all His Love, My Brothers and Sisters. And we go to give freely to all as we have received."

See your self... receiving this review of the Golden Rule as a rule for *all* humanity. Our Teacher desires for this Rule to rule all of humanity or He would not bring the Rule for review. Obedience to this Rule insures peace. No more wars of any kind? How simple the solution!

July 6
A Clear Path To Tread

"You clothe yourselves in the garments of peace and love and joy and happiness, and by your example others *will* follow.

You know you are loved. You have no doubt of this fact now. You have released your captives through your forgiveness. Yes, the hurts and stings will still come to you along the Path until all have learned the rules of our Father's Will on earth, My children.

But we have set out on the journey and others will all learn the rules from your example."

*See your self...*daily practicing the Father's Will with the express intention of setting the best example for all who share the Path with you on this great adventure.

July 7
His Love Is Sufficient

"The Path never varies. Ah, the mysteries will vary – that you must expect on this great adventure named life. But you will never vary from these simple rules of our Father's Will.

Forgiveness is His Way. You sow the seeds of Love and you will reap the harvest of peace. You know the Path full well now that we tread together. You know how to live, as He would have you live.

We will review the rules from time to time. But be assured that these rules for all our days together will never change. And you will never weary of the hearing of them.

Comfort yourselves in His Love. It *never* fails. You have all His Love and it is sufficient for all your needs."

See your self... comforted by our Father's Perfect Love for all His children. His Love will *never* fail. Is there really any greater comfort than His unfailing Love? Absolutely not!

July 8
The Gift Of Good Cheer

"Now for today! I will remind you once again that this day is a beautiful gift.

Gather the abundance of the Garden. There are those who await your smile and gentle touch. Ah, and a kind word here and there? Of course! You have a heart full of kindness to give away today.

You are becoming content with the Path now. You have no need to vary the Plan. It suits you well, My Brothers and Sisters. You are the children of His Kingdom and His Will is all you desire."

See your self... as a His laborer, preparing the soil daily for His earthly garden. His Intention for this garden is long awaited and, indeed, long overdue, but nonetheless, this earthly Paradise is assured through all your gardening skills.

July 9
Grow In Patience

"Do not become impatient with the Path. If I were to express to you My greatest desire for your life today it would be that you grow in patience.

That is your greatest need, My beloved Brothers and Sisters. You lack patience especially with your selves. Yes, and you expect far too much of each other also.

Your high expectations have caused you much unhappiness. If you are to be My disciples then you must develop this character trait of patience.

Patience is learned in the trials along the Path. And each day has sufficient trials to develop patience. You have trudged this Path long enough to know this great truth."

> *See your self...*growing in patience. It is your greatest need and scripture promises often that *every* need will be supplied.

July 10
Trust Our Father's Will

"Now I would ask you to simply trust our Father's Will for today. Trust His Will completely.

I have told you that I take your hand each day. That is also a great truth. Now trust in this truth completely. And trust that if I say you have the need to grow in patience, then the necessary trials will present themselves in your days.

But rest assured, Father is in total control. You will never receive anything in any day that we cannot handle together. Trust fully in My never-ending love. I care for you like no other can ever care.

These words are truth and they should bring you great joy and happiness. You can depend fully on Me."

> *See your self...*hand in hand with the Creator of our universe, stepping boldly forward into this day without fear or worry. His Love is unending and is yours forevermore.

July 11
The Perfect Plan

"Think of how far we have come. Yes, we have a long way yet to go, but consider what we have accomplished thus far! And today I add another little rule for the road. Fear not! Fear nothing! The Plan is perfect.

Your faith is sometimes stretched in the trust of the Plan. Ah, but you grow in faith also, My Brothers and Sisters. Indeed, the Plan is perfect for your growth. And you *will* blossom far beyond your own expectations."

See your self...fully accepting this new rule to our curriculum. Fear not! Fear no thing, and trust fully in the Perfection of our Father's Plan. Let not your heart be troubled, and never be afraid becomes the by-word for each and every day.

July 12
High Expectations

"Release your brothers and sisters from your high expectations. I have told you that you place too much of a burden on them by expecting far too much from them. They, too, struggle on the Path as you so often do.

My children, Our Father Himself does not have unreasonable expectations. The Path can be difficult enough without your adding to anyone's personal difficulties."

See your self...taking a little extra time this morning before you leave this morning's prayer closet to contemplate how these Words apply to you and your personal expectations of others on this Path? And have you placed some high form of expectation on your Self?

July 13
Need To Please

"You must not expect perfection from any brother or sister. Release them all from the need to please you.

They struggle with much the same difficulties that you struggle with this very day. They do not take their own failures well. They are as hard on themselves as you are on your Self. You smile. Of course this is the truth.

You want so very much to be happy. You constantly seek this elusive happy state. I tell you now that a valuable key to your happiness lies in the simple principle to release all your brothers and sisters from your need for them to live up to your standards."

See your self...with the potential for happiness. Could the answer to a continual happy state be as simple as releasing your need for perfection from those who surround you? Why not try to put this principle into practice? Begin this very day.

July 14
Acceptance, Allowance

"Rise early and do a little weeding in your own garden each day. Has someone hurt your feelings? Forgive them now. Cast your eyes about your garden. Has someone disappointed you? Have they failed to live up to some imaginary standard that you yourself could not attain? Release them.

Accept! Allow! Yes, allow others to simply evolve along the Path as you are evolving. Let Our Father alone provide the necessary impetus for their growth. You have plenty of labor to occupy you today in your own gardens.

Even so, you can plant the seeds of love everywhere. Yes, My children, you can plant seeds of love everywhere you go."

*See your self...*forgiving all the hurts and disappointments from the past. Why carry these burdens any further? Simply see Our Father's Path as Perfect and move steadily forward.

July 15
Our Summer Fun

"I have said that this little prayer room where you and I meet each day is to become a garden. Align your thoughts with Mine, My Brothers and Sisters, before you step forward into this beautiful day. *Now* clothe yourselves in His Love. Fill all the pockets of your hearts to overflowing with the Father's Love and get ready for the sowing labors of today.

You have much to do today as we go about our Father's Business. How many places today can you visit that will be made better for your having been there? It is a good question for you to ask yourselves as you travel abroad this day."

*See your self...*concentrating on this imperative question. How many will be blessed with the Father's Love this very day by your active participation in our Father's Business? This family Business should always be our great concern. Do be His good employee today.

July 16
You Are My Disciples

"How many love seeds will you personally plant in the Father's Kingdom? And remember always, every place you put your foot belongs to Him.

Walk the Path this day in His Love. All your sowing labors are for Him, for you labor towards the "Paradise of His Intent." You are My disciples, and yes, My beloved Brothers and Sisters, *all* is very well, Indeed!"

See your self... working in the Father's Business, ever mindful of the Paradise possible with the sowing of His Love seeds. It is a very worthy labor for His disciples and you number in that highly favored group.

July 17
Love One Another

"Today let us simply review the rule; you are to love one another each and every day from this day forward. This simple rule *must* remain central to your thinking.

Whenever you are troubled with negative thoughts, those thoughts that rob you of joy, simply ask these questions. Who have I failed to love today? Who is it that I have not extended the gentle touch of love? Who among my Brothers and Sisters have I refused a few kind words?

Once you have discovered who this sad and love-starved Brother or Sister is, simply restore this one to the garden of your loving thoughts, where we await them in His Love."

See your self... restoring all who might be standing outside our Father's amazing fellowship of love. There is a garden of Love and we are all the gardeners. Remove every weedy thought against our Father's command to Love one another as He most certainly loves us. That is our rule for all our days.

July 18
Circle Of Love

"Refuse no one the sowing of your love seeds of loving-kindness. Keep no one standing outside your love circle, My Brothers and Sisters.

You have a labor for our Father each and every day. If you call yourselves

My disciples then you must work with Me to gather all of His Children into His Kingdom of Love.

Weed your gardens and sow your seeds. These are the rules that must remain ever central for His loving Ambassadors.

Do not hurry forward each day. The Kingdom is advanced slowly but surely, one forward step at a time. Be patient, My Brothers and Sisters. The Kingdom *is* advanced one lost Child at a time."

> *See your self*...seeking and perhaps finding, this very day, one little lost child, lonely and love starved, so in need of our Father's loving grace. His Ambassadors seek every opportunity to advance our Father's Kingdom, one child at a time.

July19
Little Lost Child

"Once you were a little lost child. Once you stumbled forward, alone and frightened and I found you. I picked you up and slowly, with patient tenderness; as a Shepherd finds His sheep, I brought you to this place, where you know you are loved and I AM with you.

And now we labor side by side to seek for those lost and love-starved children, who desperately need to know of Our Father's unconditional love for each and every one of them. We seek these children one by one."

> *See your self*...laboring side by side with our good Shepherd, ever seeking the lonely and the lost children needful of Our Father's unconditional love.

July 20
Slowly But Surely

"You will do all that is required in this day. You have a simple task. Extend the love that you have received. Go about the ordinary tasks of this day ever ready to extend His Hand of Love to all that cross your Path.

Father will send the lost to you. They will be ready to receive all you have to give. There is never a lack, nor is there ever a lack of places for the sowing of our Father's precious love seeds. You will know exactly what you must do and you will gladly do what must be done."

*See your self...*prepared to do all that is required to do this day. Father will send those with the lack of love that you must be ever ready to supply.

July 21
The Power To Heal

"Let us concentrate now on love's power to heal, My Beloveds. All of this world's dis-ease is the effect of mankind's inability to love one another. That is why I bring this one central rule of His Kingdom to your remembrance so often. "Love one another."

My children, It is a simple principle to learn; Love heals. And forgiveness is the medicine, the love balm that is the impetus for the healing of your world. Day by day we go forward to disperse this great healing medicine."

*See your self...*as a healer, dispensing love as a healing medicine. You have the power within to add immeasurably to the healing of so very much of this world's "dis-ease" and great discomfort.

July 22
Most Worthy Cause

"Do not be discouraged by the negative reports you receive. Listen to My Voice. I will tell you again and again these great words of encouragement. The Kingdom of our Father's Intent *will* come, and that is no idle fantasy. You do not labor in vain. Love changes everything, My Beloveds.

Your daily acts of kindness are not small or useless endeavors. Every kind act, every single kind word, however small or insignificant you may think it to be, advances His Kingdom. Love will heal the universe It is a most worthy cause you serve each day.

Continue with your labors, your efforts to do His Will! You do well! Yes, His Love changes everything!"

*See your self...*laboring daily to advance Father's heavenly Kingdom on earth. His Kingdom will come and remember always that "is no idle fantasy."

July 23
The Habit Of Impatience

"Think now of your own unhappiness. You desire to walk in love, however you have some habits that need changing. Let us begin a little clean up process. Let us begin a new work.

I will remind you now of the habit of impatience, yes, with yourselves and also with one another. Impatience with others instills fear and frustration. Impatience indicates that you know better than anyone, even better than God, when and how life should take place.

We are going to concentrate on making a change in a habit you really no longer need to carry with you. Impatience is a most unnecessary burden.

To combat this unfortunate habit and alleviate its negative effects, let us begin with one simple helpful action. Slow down! I have told you before that there is no hurry."

*See your self...*as impatient, yes, but willing to lay this unnecessary burden down. It's a difficult habit to break but you can do it. Make an effort today to be more patient with all those you meet on the Path and perhaps even allowing your Self the grace for a little leeway in this formidable area.

July 24
Remember To Breathe

"Right now, before we go any further into our day, simply take a few very deep breaths. Inhale slowly, then exhale, and then again.

Impatience begins with an irritation and very often very quickly escalates to anger. It will amaze you how often the whole downhill process can be totally alleviated by simply taking the time to deeply breathe.

Stop often to breathe deeply, and begin to focus more fully now on the times each day when you do find yourselves in a situation of grave impatience.

Find a little place to come away with Me. In the moments of chaos, learn to think on our Friendship. It is like no other."

*Se your Self...*taking these precious words into today.
"Think on our Friendship. It is like no other."

July 25
Poor Habits

"Today, think again, My beloved Brothers and Sisters, of how impatient you are.

You hurry about, and the slightest difficulty that takes you away from your appointed schedule makes you angry.

Anger is a habit birthed in impatience. By developing a more patient attitude, you will remove anger from your poor habit list.

Now I ask you quite simply, does anger or impatience ever really change your difficult situations? No! Both anger and impatience stop your progress towards the solutions."

See your self ...taking our Teacher's excellent advice to breathe deeply; inhale slowly and exhale slowly, and then again. Ah, can you establish a new habit to annihilate the old impatience and anger habit of long standing? Try it! There is nothing to lose and everything to gain.

July 26
The Anger Habit

"Yes, Anger is a habit! I would say that you have become *addicted* to anger. You believe you gain control over your circumstances, the unwanted circumstances of this life journey, with anger.

Now I tell you to simply accept the fact that life will not always go your way. You know this is the truth.

Difficulties are a part, a very natural and intrinsic part of growth. Almost daily you will encounter difficulty. That is why you must properly adjust your thinking towards the elimination of impatience and the poor habit of responding with anger.

Review these words again before you leave our little morning meeting. They will make perfect sense."

See your self ...reviewing these words again and admitting to your Self that indeed, these words make perfect sense. Ah, if only we all could eliminate impatience and the very poor habit of responding to life's difficulties with anger.

July 27
Be Patient With The Process

"We will be very busy this season. It is time for some changes. It is time to take some great forward steps.

Be patient with the process, My beloved children. We will move forward and accomplish much together. We will face many challenges together and we will greet them all with the knowing that our Father has placed every challenge on our Path for our absolute good.

Do you feel perhaps that our curriculum intensifies? Of course it does! You are ready to move to a higher level. You are ready to learn all that our Father wills for this place on the Path of our progress."

See your self...accepting the daily challenges with perhaps more enthusiasm for the growth promised in every challenge. The curriculum *will* take you to a higher level of growth. Challenges assure growth.

July 28
Mountains Into Molehills

"For He causes *all* things to work for good."

These words from My servant Paul ring true across the centuries. Think carefully on the word "all." Everything, *all* challenges are for your growth.

And know that we *will* work together to make better choices in the challenges that appear. And these challenges will appear often. And they are *all* programmed for your growth. You must remember that *every* challenge must be met with patience and with love. And now I will tell you to learn this lesson well.

If you choose to meet every challenge with patience and with love, you will change the mountain of every challenge into the proverbial molehill. You can say to every mountain "be removed" and it will be removed. We can do this together."

*See your self...*working "together" with our Teacher and our great Friend, and yes, turning all our mountains of challenge into clearly removable obstacles to our Path.

July 29
Meet Every Challenge

"There are challenges to be met today, My beloved children. Sometimes you know when you arise that the day ahead will be filled with difficulty, and sometimes one of the greatest challenges is just getting out of bed.

I know that life isn't easy for many of you, My dear ones. But we go in faith each day, in the knowledge that we can meet *every* challenge. The Path we tread is ever upward and we are progressing."

*See your self...*accepting with joy the good news for today. We *can* meet every challenge and we are progressing. Ah, yes, that is such very good news from our Friend and great Companion on the Path.

July 30
You Are Learning

"You are learning to love one another. You are learning to forgive and bear no grudges. You do take fewer mental burdens into each day. And you have become far more kind and gentle in your words and actions.

Now in retrospect, with just this little morning review, you see the definite forward progress. Learning to meet every challenge with patience and love will take time.

So I repeat today, there is no hurry. And you have taken a great forward step with the simple understanding that every challenge can be met with patience and love."

See your self...with far less mental burdens, accepting a slower pace for the Path. There is no need to hurry. You are learning all that is necessary for continual progress.

July 31
I And My Father Are One

"You will grow accustomed to our Father's loving Will as we progress together. And one day your will, in truth, will be one with His. And you will say these words with Me, "I and My Father are one." And you will say them in perfect truth and with perfect understanding."

See your self...arriving one day to a place of perfect truth and perfect understanding; a place where your will and our Father's Will "are one" in perfect union.

AUGUST

August 1
The Ministry Of Love

"A new day lies before us. You are well into the day already. You hold no one in the debt of unforgiveness. You are clothing yourselves right now, as we meet, in the uniform of our Father's Service. You are ready to meet every brother and sister with the gift of our Father's unconditional love. You are well on your way for the ministry of love.

Now step courageously forward into this day. Our work begins the moment you leave this quiet meeting. But know full well that you go into the day with all the help you need for all the tasks you face however difficult they may seem."

*See your self...*stepping into this day with courage knowing you have all the help your need for all that is required for you to accomplish. You are His ministers of love.

August 2
Change The World

"You can do much to change the world. I have told you before that love changes everything. Every act of kindness, however small, is a step towards paradise on earth. Think of this often. Think thoughts of love and how you personally can make a purposeful attempt each day to sow seeds of love. And do not forget to weed the seeds of negativity.

Meet with Me each day, for it is My intention to teach you how to love. This is a great undertaking. We are out to change the world from darkness into light. You are My little lamplighters. You will create a great light, one light at a time, until all His Children are living and loving in Our Father's Perfect Will."

See your self...as His Lamplighters daily involved in the great undertaking of sowing seeds of Love.

August 3
You Can Make A Difference

"I will speak to you often, My Beloveds, of our Father's Will. He desires simply that you love one another. Little acts of kindness will certainly change the world one kind act at a time.

You can individually make a great difference. Never believe for one minute that you are not an important part of Father's perfect Plan. Remind yourselves that there is no greater labor than the labor in our Father's Will on earth."

See your self...advancing our Father's earthy Kingdom this very day, with all your little acts of kindness. You do play a very important part in His perfect Plan.

August 4
Whom You Serve Each Day

"The day before us will offer many opportunities for you to love one another. Take the time to assure yourselves that you are, indeed, in a worthy service as you go about our Father's Business.

You will serve Him well today with your smiles and gentle touches and the simple acts of kindness that you perform throughout your day to bring the healing light of love to all mankind. You are the Ambassadors of His Light and Love.

Take a few minutes to simply center your thinking on Whom you serve each day."

See your self...as Father sees you. You are His Ambassador of Light and Love. There is no greater service.

August 5
Center Your Intention On Love

"I thank you for meeting with Me each morning. We go together to co-create "the Paradise of our Father's Intent."

Yes, it is our Father's Will that all His children love one another, and the spreading of His perfect Will throughout the universe begins with you, My Beloved Brothers and Sisters.

You must center your intention always on Love. Be kind. Be gentle to each and every Brother and Sister that you meet today. They all face great challenges as each of you do, but their many burdens are greatly reduced by your kindness and gentleness to each and every one of them."

See your self...co-creating "the Paradise of our Father's Intent." Some may view the biblical "garden of Paradise" as pure myth, but we do not. Love always makes paradise a reality.

August 6
Hear My Gentle Promptings

"Be very sure that you focus on this task early in each day. Perhaps My Words to you seem repetitious, but the words of His Love Service bear repeating often. You serve a grand and very glorious cause.

You are here to learn to love. For many of you this is not easy. You have grave hurts and emotional pains to overcome. But you will do well, My Brothers and Sisters.

You know you are moving forward. And you also know that I go with you. You know we can accomplish much together. We have already come far.

Just listen to the prompting of the Spirit within you. You will hear My gentle prompting often. Simply follow the call to love. Learn to quiet your minds.

The still small Voice is *always* there, wooing gently, asking you to bring all the love within you to the waiting world that surrounds you."

*See your self...*ever listening, tuned into the Spirit's gentle prompting. Love is your mission. And you will not fail.

August 7
Consistent And Persistent

"I have asked you to center your thinking on the good and to forget *all* the negative reports of the world's condition. Do not be discouraged with the evil reports. I tell you the truth. You have the Power of Love to heal *all* this world's seeming evil.

All is well with your own hearts and minds this day. You can change the negative to the positive in *every* situation with simple acts of love.

Smile often. You will see a new lightness in your own burdens if you take the time to lighten someone else's.

Step forward with a smile on your face and the Love of our Father brimming over from your hearts and minds, and be prepared for a mighty swell of goodness. Be consistent and persistent to love all your brothers and sisters. Good *will* triumph! You are on the Path to Glory."

See your self...smiling often throughout this day. Enjoy the word "Good will triumph! And you are a co-partner in all the good that will brighten your Path today.

August 8
Words That Bear Repeating

"You are My children, and My Father's children, birthed in love and great light. We go forward together today to spread the Love of God. It is a noble task that we set about to perform. There is no greater service to mankind than the service of His Love to one another.

You *will* change the world, with one loving act a time, in the daily service of Our Father's Love Brigade. You are Soldiers in the mighty Army that ventures forward daily with the Healing Balm of Love. And I AM with you."

See your self...changing this world in partnership with none other than the great I AM. There is no greater service or partnership than this one we all share with Him.

August 9
Good Will Triumph

"Yes, good will triumph, My Beloved Children. I know that sometimes this is difficult to believe. The world seems to reel about in chaos. But No! Father has total control in *all* things. Nothing is ever outside of His Control. And He sends you forward each day to balance the chaotic conditions."

*See your self...*as His balancing factor in the chaos of life's Path. He has chosen wisely all those who serve in this worthy task.

August 10
Learn To Listen

"Early in the morning before you begin, find a quiet place to meet with us. We are always waiting to enfold you in our embrace. And again in the evening, come away with us for a few moments of rest from your travels. These are the pauses in life that truly refresh and revive you.

You will learn to still your mind and listen for directions. You will hone your listening skills, My Brothers and Sisters. Learning to listen for directions is a very important part of our daily curriculum. Daily seek a few minutes of stillness now and then as you go about your day."

*See your self...*learning to listen as a very important part of our curriculum. Seeking times of stillness leaves a proverbial "door open" to hear the necessary instructions.

August 11
Spiritual Solace

"The morning meetings are to prepare you for the Path and the evening meetings will bring you comfort and solace.

Learn to come away, My Beloved Brothers and Sisters. Learn to seek these comforting times alone with us. You will *never* regret developing the habit of these meetings. Seek these precious moments in our company. They will revive and refresh you as nothing else. Yes, revival is yours with every meeting.

There is such great spiritual solace in our daily meetings. And indeed,

---

you need this solace. It is as important to your progress as the air you breathe and the food you eat."

See your self...developing the habit of these precious daily meetings. You need these meetings. You need daily refreshment and revival.

August 12
Precious Moments

"I have told you, My Beloved Brothers and Sisters, that these precious moments in our company will revive and refresh you as nothing else. Know that this is an absolute truth. There is nothing in your day as important as your coming away from your daily tasks to spend some quiet time with us.

You are learning to love one another. You are learning to quiet your thinking and to listen to My Voice.

You will continue now for all the days of your lives in this wonderful program that will, in time, benefit all mankind. It is a simple task, is it not, to simply come away each day to establish order in the chaos?"

See your self...learning to quiet your mind enabling you to hear our Beloved's Voice. These quiet moments will establish order in the chaos.

August 13
Seek And You Shall Find

"You are Our Father's Children. You yearn for order. You know there is only one way to the peace that all humankind seeks. It begins in your own heart and mind.

You must seek the peace within. And I have said, "Seek and you shall find." You will establish great order in your own chaos. You will set the tides of peace in your own little world by simply loving every single Brother and Sister in your Path each day. And day-by-day your little endeavors will grow and magnify, spilling over into all the little worlds of your Brothers and Sisters."

*See your self...*creating peace in your own heart and mind. Then expect that your peace *will* spill over into the hearts and minds of those who share the Path with you each day.

August 14
Love Is An Action

"The goal is one world of Love. And it will come. You will not fail. Father's Plan is perfect. Listen each day and do your part. Your part is important to our Father's Plan, My Beloveds. Yes, the world is filled with Father's Children, all beautiful in His Sight. Never forget how beautiful each of you really are in His Eyes."

*See your self...*as our Father's beautiful child, surrounded on every side by all of His other beautiful Children, every Child beautiful and very precious in His Sight.

August 15
Tender Your Garden

"It has been a while now since we talked of you as tenders of His Garden. But I will remind you today of your gardening tasks. You are here to plant the seeds of love. You do not need to be reminded to remove the weeds of negativity.

You know full well now that you can control your thinking. I will remind you often of the importance of the love seeds, and also of your importance to His Plan for world peace.

You hear of the world's ambassadors of world peace and you have realized so often that, indeed, they are all talk and no action.

Let Me remind you today of a simple fact. Love is an action. Love is not a feeling. Love is not just a word. It requires work. Some of you know full well that love is difficult in some instances. You know you must put forth some effort. I will work with you."

> *See your self...*as His Love Ambassadors and laborers in His Garden. Be ready this very day to put forth whatever effort it takes, to plant the necessary love seeds that will lead to peace.

August 16
Your Are Co-Creators

"It is our Father's Will, My Beloveds, that His Love be shed abroad through all the Universes. Like pollen on the wings of the wind, you are His Instruments. You are His Chosen Ones. He delights in every one of your endeavors to create the beautiful gardens of His Will on earth.

You are here as co-creators to bring all this earth to the great beauty of His Intention. You serve a mighty cause indeed! Do not lose sight *ever* of the importance of your personal part in His Perfect Plan.

Each day you are to perform acts of love. You are to be kind and gentle and ever ready to extend His Hand through yours in Love. This is the Plan."

> *See your self...*creating a constant love environment. He holds your hand in His, and you and He are the co-creators of every love action extended freely to all who cross your Path each day.

August 17
We Are A Team

"Today is a beautiful day! You may feel rushed as the duties of this day call you forward. But *always* take the time to come away to settle into the mode of operation for each day.

You know that we go with you as a little team in a field of countless teams with the singular purpose of our Father's Will.

There is a great unity in this Brotherhood of Love and we are advancing daily in the goal of peace on earth.

It seems a small part that you play, but I assure you today, there are truly no small parts. Every Child is important. Every Brother and Sister is needed to complete His Purpose. Love is His Purpose. And love and peace are one."

*See your self...*an active participant, unified in love with all your Brothers and Sisters. Remember always, Love is His Purpose for *all* the days of your earthly existence.

August 18
Love At The Center

"Our Father's Purpose, My Beloveds, is Love. His greatest desire is that you learn to love one another. Yes, learning to love is our curriculum. You may say that love is the title of our Course. Place love at the center, the focal point of all your actions.

If you are not walking in love, you are not in the Father's Perfect Will. Measure your day's progress by all your loving actions. Unloving actions are counterproductive always."

*See your self...*paying close attention daily to the love curriculum. You are a good student. Avoid all that is counterproductive to the Father's Perfect Will.

August 19
Tend With Mercy

"You are making progress, My beloved Brothers and Sisters. You are learning to forgive quickly the little hurts and painful incidents that happen to each of you along life's path. Forgive quickly, for unforgiveness puts its ugly roots deep within your emotions.

You need to ask yourself each morning if there is anyone in need of your mercy. You must tend your gardens well. The weeds of negativity are constantly spoiling the beauty that could be yours with some careful attention to your thoughts.

Be ever on guard against negativity. It takes a heavy toll. You know this is truth. You go forth to create great beauty in His Love. It should delight your hearts to serve in this mighty cause of our Father's Will on earth. Tend with mercy."

*See your self...*forgiving *every* hurt and painful incident. Try to do this as quickly as is humanly possible. Why carry the very unnecessary burden of unforgiveness? Why, Indeed!

August 20
Wear A Smile

"Again, I remind you of the garb you wear each day. A smile, a gentle touch, a kind and loving word or action now and then, mark you as Our Father's children.

And you are easily recognized now as His children. There is no doubt whatsoever that you serve our Father's Will. You are certain that you are making progress. You know you have come far in these past few months. You also know you have yet far to go."

*See your self...*dressing each day in the garb of His heavenly Kingdom on earth. Smiles, gentle touches, coupled with kind words and loving actions make us all easily recognized as His Children.

August 21
We Will Guide You

"You need to be reminded often, My Beloveds, of Father's Will that you love one another. Keep this simple rule of action always in the forefront of your thinking.

Let love be the banner, His Banner that waves over each and every one of His Children. He loves you *all* with such a tender love, like no other you could ever experience. And assuredly, He desires your total happiness.

I will help you. I promise to be a good tutor throughout all the days of your life. Listen to My Voice. I will guide you daily on the Path. If you come to a place where love is a labor, then remember Whom you serve this day. And remember always that We go with you constantly into the sowing fields."

*See your self...*accepting this incredible "promise" for guidance in every need as you journey forward into the "sowing fields" of His eternal Love.

August 22
Weeds Of Negativity

"You must learn to control your negative emotions. They are simply habits of long standing. You have spent your entire lifetime in the practice of negative thinking.

It is not easy to break a long-standing habit. It takes a great deal of concentration. But there are such marvelous rewards for your diligence.

Persist in the removal of the weeds of negativity. At the root of all these negative weeds is the failure to love one another. Examine every thought that robs you of your happiness. Concentrate on the joy-robbing thoughts and you will invariably find a Brother or Sister who needs your mercy and love. Plant seeds of love in this garden!

Put a smile on your face today. A simple smile, freely given, is a grand insignia marking you as the servants of Our Father's Will on earth."

See your self...smiling often today. And do the necessary gardening chore of removing all the weeds of negativity and every joy-robbing thought.

August 23
Break The Habit

"Yes, My Brothers and Sisters, you may be assured that I AM your tutor. I will help you break the habit of negative thinking. Be totally aware that all your thoughts are your choice. You are not the victim of your negative thinking.

Yes, negative circumstances can arise. You cannot avoid all negative situations. But you can adjust your thinking as to how you handle them. I will help you. I promise to be a good tutor throughout all the days of your life. Listen to My Voice. I will guide you daily on the Path."

See your self...as a daily student to the great I AM. Accept His repeated powerful promise to be your tutor throughout all of your life experience.

August 24
Fear Is Lack Of Trust

"All negative thinking is fear-based. You become fearful so easily, My Beloveds. Fear is lack of trust. You know that your Father unconditionally loves you and He would never cause anything to harm you.

Now, let us begin to erase the false teaching that your Father wishes to punish His Children for their supposed mistakes and errors along the Path. Yes, the scriptures contain man's thinking. Man believes in God's punishment for mistakes and errors. That is not our Father's Way. Love is His Answer, never pain and suffering. We begin today to correct this negative thinking."

> *See your self*...trusting that our Father would never harm us or purposely cause any of His children pain and suffering. His unconditional Love promises us freedom from the doom and gloom of mankind's irrational thinking.

August 25
The Apex Of Negativity

"Ah, yes, the fear of hell is the apex of negativity. There is no hell; the doctrine of hell is a lie. If you believe in this false doctrine, then you do not believe that our Father loves all His Children. I have told you that He loves you. And if you believe in hell then you do not believe My words. For what kind of love is it that could create a place like hell, a place to contain God's Children in pain and suffering for all eternity?

Why would our Father ask you to forgive one another if *He* could not forgive each and every one of you? Why would He ask of you something He could not do Himself? God is love. He cannot not love."

> *See your self*...living fearlessly by releasing the doctrine of eternal damnation for any of God's eternally loved

Children. There is a place prepared for punishment but only for "the devil and his fallen angels." Are you God's Child? Then Fear not!

August 26
God's Love Is Unconditional

"God is Love. He loves unconditionally. And Love does not create hell. Hell is man's creation, and you must lay aside this insane thinking. There is no greater lie than that of eternal punishment.

Father holds no child in the captivity of unforgiveness. Love forgives all. Love holds no grudges. Love is patient. Love is kind. Love is full of mercy. And love understands *Everything*. There is no room for the insanity of hell in Love.

You go forth to create great beauty in His Love. It should delight your hearts to serve in this mighty cause of Father's Will on earth."

See your self...learning to love as Father Loves. Unconditional love will change the world.

August 27
Life and Love Are Eternal

"Death has no promise to capture you for all eternity. Love awaits your crossing. Life is eternal, as is Love. You are eternally loved and that is the truth. You may rest assured in His eternal love for each and every one of you.

My beloved Brothers and Sisters, there is no fear in death if there is no hell. You need fear nothing about the crossing over from this life to the next. It is a gentle transition from life to life. Lay aside today all fear. Fear nothing whatsoever in leaving this earth place for the eternal shores."

*See your self...*as a fearless child, resting forevermore in our Father's priceless love. Yes, this promise is assured. Love awaits your crossing from this life to the next.

August 28
The Best Is Yet To Come

"I tell you the truth when I say to you to fear nothing. Too much time has been wasted, My Brothers and Sisters, on fear. You are the beloved Children of our most beloved Father. His Plans for your future are good. You can be very sure that the best is yet to come.

Eternal life is His Perfect Plan for all His children. Eternal life is the apex of His Creation. You can be sure that the eternal shores are a delight beyond anything you could ever imagine as delightful.

I have told you these things to bring you peace in the turmoil of your days. There is no darkness in eternal life. There is only peace, love and joy abundant. Father's Plans for you are very good. Rest assured today in this great truth."

*See your self...*facing the future in great confidence that Father's Plans for your life experience "are very good." Ah, Indeed, such a great truth and worthy of reviewing often.

August 29
Perfect Peace

"Yes, My beloved Brothers and Sister, I have said that our Father's plans for you are very good. Be in perfect peace about your future days. We are in this together. You will have all the help you need to accomplish all that Father's plan entails for each and every one of you.

These days ahead will be very full. There will be those days when you will wonder if you will have enough strength for all the tasks at hand. But you will always have the strength you need. You are on a perfect Path."

> *See your self*...in perfect peace today. You are on a perfect path. And you will have the help you need for all that you need to accomplish. You know Who goes with you every step of the Way.

August 30
God Is Our Provider

"Father is very aware of *all* your needs. And He will abundantly provide for His Will in your progress. Yes, center your thinking on these words, "His Will for your progress." We need concern ourselves with no other will but His. You will grow very accustomed to following the Inner Voice, ever leading you towards His Will and only His. To love one another will become your will, too.

Now today fill again the pockets of your hearts with seeds of love. And move about your day with the personal choice for the extension of your hand in love. And be prepared to be kind to every Brother and Sister you meet."

> *See your self*...advancing daily in Father's curriculum of love. It is Father's Will that you make consistent progress in His Perfect Plan. Your love and kindness to every Brother and Sister is His love and kindness through you.

August 31
Live In Today

"The Path provides you with many lessons. You do not know the answers to all the questions of life's varied curriculum. And you perceive that you have often failed the testing of life's trials. This is not the truth. Again I tell you that you are far too hard on yourselves. You should give yourselves far more credit for the lessons already learned.

You are growing in you understanding of the principles of cause and effect. And you know that you must take responsibility for the growth of your own souls.

Enjoy today! Be happy in His never-ending care for you. Rejoice and live happily in His abundant Love. Fear not!"

See your self... making daily progress in the provided lessons. Perhaps you might take a minute to give yourself credit for the good work you have accomplished thus far. It's been an excellent month for the advancement of Father's Kingdom Principles. You are an excellent servant to His Will.

SEPTEMBER

September 1
In His Image

"Good morning, My precious Children, and welcome to our quiet time together. We approach a new season.

The lessons, though difficult sometimes, are all necessary. You must ever advance; ever ascend, even as you must learn to live in today.

Forget the errors of the past. You will be given another chance, and always then again another, and another if necessary, to make better choices.

You are maturing. You are learning from the trials and errors. You are growing daily toward the visible image of our Father in each and every one of you. You are learning to love in His Name and in His wonderful Will for all His Children. And I say to you all today, He is very pleased with your progress."

> *See your self*...learning all the valuable lessons in every trial and error. You are maturing. And yes, our Father is very pleased with your progress. This is no idle fantasy.

September 2
In His Name

"Now as we begin this new day, My Beloveds, let Me remind you again that you have a purpose in this day. You are learning to love in His wonderful Name.

Yes, sometimes it is an effort to love one another. For as many times as I remind you that Father bears no grudges against any of His Children, you must be reminded to bear no grudges against any of your Brothers and Sisters.

This is not an easy lesson, for many of you bear the scars of a lifetime of pain and suffering. And it is not easy to let that suffering go. But you must.

For in the release of anyone you hold captive to unforgiveness, is your own release to personal freedom."

*See your self...*fully accepting our Father's total forgiveness of all your errors and mistakes, past, present and yes, future. Then in like manner, release any captives to unforgiveness that remain in your life experience, past, present and future. Be free!

September 3
Love Unfettered

"From time to time, I remind you of the forgiveness prayer. Pause a moment right now. Is there anyone you need to forgive? If so, then simply do it. Take no burdens into this beautiful day. It is as simple as saying "I forgive." And in the mercy and love of these beautiful words, you are ready to face the new day in the freedom of love unfettered.

Now go and receive whatever lessons are prepared for your part in the growth towards the paradise of our Father's Intention. And remind yourselves often of the wonder of serving as Ambassadors to His Will on this good earth."

See your self...using the forgiveness prayer today if necessary. Your work as His Ambassador requires your freedom from the burden of unforgiveness.

September 4
Sunshine Of His Love

"Today is a beautiful gift, My Beloved Brothers and Sisters. Allow the sunshine of our Father's Love to warm your hearts, and, as you go forward, be prepared to extend that warmth to everyone who comes into your life today.

Take a few minutes to prepare your minds for the Service of His Kingdom's Growth. Your love will be tested, for you are asked to serve all your Family in the love of His wonderful Name.

Yes, there will be challenges that we all must meet today, but Love's Light will shine on every challenge."

See your self...allowing His Love Light to shine brightly through you today and every day.

September 5
Our Family

"No Brother or Sister is excluded from our family. That is the reason you are called to labor in the service of His Will on earth. We serve a truly marvelous cause. We are to bring the unity of His Love to all mankind. Always recognize the importance of *your part* in the service of His Will on earth.

Now prepare yourselves with the simple desire to serve in whatever manner is provided. He has planned today and all your days for the advancement of love. Be joyful in your part, for you are here to bring great joy and peace."

See your self...always as His Ambassador of great joy and peace.

September 6
Cause And Effect

"The fruit of love is peace, My Brothers and Sisters. You will learn to enjoy the fruits of your labors each day. In the failure to love all your Brothers and Sisters, there is most assuredly the absence of peace.

This is the apex of the cause and effect principle. When there is a lack of peace in your life, there is a need for you to examine the cause.

The effect of your failure at loving one another is *always* the lack of peace. Our Father's Will is denied every time you fail to love one another.

Our Father's Children are recognized easily by the spirit of their kind and gentle attitudes. Continue to bless your world with happiness by your happy attitudes.

You must think on these words today and decide if peace is worth the labor of love."

See your self...easily recognized as our Father's child. Peace is worth all your efforts to maintain a kind and gentle attitude.

September 7
More Than Pretty Words

"You do not take sufficient time to think on our lessons each day. These lessons are more than just pretty words. We are not together in this time for Me to tickle your ears endlessly with how very much our Father loves each and every one of you. Won't you simply accept this great truth and go forward in His Service?

There is much to accomplish in His Will. The cause of love always brings the effect of peace and when you have no peace, you have failed the Father's Cause. Remember these words as you go abroad with your daily tasks. Remember it is always His Cause you serve."

*See your self...*selflessly serving His Cause. Daily make His Will your will.

September 8
Rudiments Of Peace

"My beloved Brothers and sisters, I am going to teach you how to bring peace into your own little world. One by one you will learn the rudiments of peace. Remember this simple principle always. There is no peace without love.

I am here with you now to help you produce the fruits of the Spirit. We will labor together all the days of your life. You will produce the fruits of love. You will see blossoms of love eventually bearing the fruit of the peace that passes understanding. And that is no idle fantasy. I know, for I AM the Prince of Peace."

*See your self...*working tirelessly together with our Beloved Prince of Peace for the furtherance of our Father's Perfect Will on earth.

September 9
Lay Down Your Swords

"What then, My Beloveds, is this peace that passes understanding? It is a peace that is maintained in the storms and trials of life. In this life you will have tribulation. You can be sure there is no escape from almost daily turmoil.

Until all your Brothers and Sisters lay down the swords of war, both the mental and physical swords, you can be certain there will be war. Ah, but you can know peace, total peace, in *every* situation that tries your spirit.

Let Me teach you how to lay down every sword of malice and anger, for indeed, this is the Pathway to Peace. Determine today to put away the swords that produce all the hate in this world."

See your self...creating a new thought life, containing no swords of malice, anger or hatred.

September 10
Implements Of War

"Perhaps you have never thought of your little daily skirmishes as preventing the peace that passes understanding from becoming all-encompassing in our Father's universe. But I tell you this truth, My Brothers and Sisters. Until every sword of anger and hatred is put aside, there will never be the peace on earth of our Father's Intention.

You must begin today to lay away your own war implements. I challenge you today to do your part. This is an important labor we undertake together. As I have said before, our Father's Children are recognized easily by the spirit of their kind and gentle attitudes. Continue to bless your world with happiness by your happy attitudes"

See your self...blessing the world that surrounds you each day, with a happy attitude. Our Teacher repeats that we are easily recognized as our Father's Children by our kind and gentle attitudes. Whatever the effort you put forward today as His Ambassador will further our Father's Intention for peace on earth.

September 11
Peace On Earth?

"Yes, My Brothers and Sisters, the Father's Business, our labor together, is to bring peace on earth. And it must begin with each one of you. You must learn to lay down every sword of anger and malice. You must individually learn to war no more. All of you can stem the tide of hatred by beginning today to do your part.

You have often thought that you could do little on your own to bring peace on earth. But I tell you now this truth. Peace begins in the inner kingdom of self. I have said that the kingdom of heaven lies within. Yet many of My Children have created little hells, personal hells, within themselves.

You must learn to release yourselves from the hells of your own making. You must learn to free yourselves from the hells of your unforgiveness. You must unlearn war."

See your self...releasing your Self from any mental hell of your own creation. Release all unforgiveness and be set free from all condemnation.

September 12
House Cleaning

"If you would have peace on earth, My Brothers and Sisters, then you must consider what it is that your part of that peace should be.

You have a little kingdom of self that needs some daily maintenance. And I would have you begin today to examine some of the swords you carry. It is your Father's desire that you reach and maintain the heavenly kingdom within. And so we begin house cleaning. It is a step-by-step process."

See your self...as a meticulous housekeeper of the inner kingdom within. The peace that passes all understanding is ever the goal of our Father's heavenly kingdom dweller.

September 13
Words Of Love

"There are a great many of our Father's beloved children who carry the sword of a razor sharp tongue. Let Me ask you today, are you one of those children? Do you too quickly cut down one of your Brothers and Sisters with the sword of your tongue?

If the answer is yes, then you know you must put that sword away. Before you leave our morning meeting, purpose in your heart today to try to lay down this sword. Ah, there is a better day ahead for each of you who attempt this one loving act alone. Of this you can be very sure.

Were all the razor sharp tongues of anger and malice put aside quickly, all wars would end in an amazingly short period of time"

See your self...purposely learning to control your tongue.
Speak words of love or speak no words at all.

September 14
Speak Only Love

"How can you ever obtain peace, My Beloveds, if you do not first lay down *all* swords of malice and anger? How then, you may ask, is this accomplished? You must learn to think before you speak. And that may well be, for most of you, the most difficult lesson in our curriculum.

The control of your tongues is a godly characteristic. Do not worry however, and please do not be hard on yourselves as from time to time you feel you fail. This is not a lesson learned in a short season, My Brothers and Sisters. You will labor long on this one little habit."

See your self...accepting the labor to conquer this habit.
Vow today to be free one day from all malice and anger.

September 15
The Unruly Member

"The tongue is a two edged sword. From this tiny body member, both disease and great healing can be accomplished. It is a great measure of your maturation if you can simply stop a moment *before you speak* and make an assessment of what you wish to accomplish with your words.

You will have victory by simply making it your continual heart's desire to *speak only love*. You can do this. I would never ask you to do anything that is not possible."

> *See your self*...as a child with great focus on making this necessary adjustment to controlling the tongue. "You can do this." You can learn to think before you speak.

September 16
"Is This Love?"

"If you can control your thoughts, My beloveds, you can control your words. And as our Father's Ambassadors, you can learn to speak words of love. You will bring great healing to this love-starved universe with love as your focus.

You know the damage each of you has received in your lifetime from brothers and sisters who did not know how to control their tongues. Malice and anger have deeply scared you all. And yes, you have done some scarring yourselves. But that all belongs to the past!

Before you damage anyone with either anger or malice, simply ask the question, "Is this love?" Let love be your focus."

> *See your self*...acknowledging the pain you have both given and received from this unruly member. If love is your focus, then the sword of the tongue must be adjusted fully to the love commandment.

September 17
Garbed In Joy

"This is a beautiful day!

Again, I remind you to garb yourselves in the joy of His Service. Smile often. Greet one another with only loving words, and make kindness your banner.

You grow quickly now in the Service of His Honor and Glory. Those who surround you on every side from the spirit kingdom applaud your every effort for the furtherance of His Perfect Will on earth.

Yes, you are learning to make better choices in this area, but you do have a long way to go till you reach total freedom."

See your self...growing daily in the freedom of no anger or malice towards anyone. You have a new peace in all your days.

September 18
Voice Of Love

"We go forth each day, My Brothers and Sisters, to cast the seeds of love into every corner of our world. It may seem sometimes a thankless task to be consistent in keeping Father's command to love one another. But you do see the fruits in this service of love. And you would have it no other way then to continue in the curriculum.

You are becoming better acquainted with the service of His Will. You are learning to forgive quickly those Brothers and Sisters who have not progressed quite so quickly as you have.

You must remember that many have not learned to seek the kingdom of heaven within. There are many voices they hear that crowd out the still small Voice of Love. And so My Brothers and Sisters, you must learn patience."

See your self...accepting with patience the Love commandment, freely giving to others the Love of God that you have so abundantly received.

September 19
Sit Quietly With Me

"Be happy for the progress you have made thus far. You do listen. And you are learning Father's universal laws.

You must simply bear with Me as I lead you daily forward. You can learn so much in the days ahead. We will take more time now to simply practice taking a few breathers in the day. Come away now and then to sit quietly with Me."

See your self...finding another time in your busy day to slip away and be with our most beloved Friend, always available and only one thought away from wherever you are and in whatever moment you may find your Self.

September 20
Come Away With Me

"Would you not seek but a few minutes later in the day to come away with Me? You have become accustomed to our morning meetings. They are now a daily habit.

But would you add another few minutes as our day progresses? Perhaps at mid-day, or the end of your work-a-day chores, you could just come away and allow Me to comfort you.

Simply trust in My love. I will always be there for you. There is no need to speak in these quiet moments. Just be still and allow us to be one in the Spirit. Find a quiet place and simply be with Me.

Connect your selves by simply saying, 'I am here to be in stillness for a few moments with my Friend and Brother.' Trust fully that whenever you mentally connect with Me, I am here.

I will always be here for you, My beloved Brothers and Sisters. I love you as no other could ever love you."

*See your self...*setting aside a few extra minutes later in your day to reconnect mentally with our amazing older and wiser Brother and Friend.

September 21
His Will Alone

"Self will is a great peace robber! You know that His Will alone is the Pathway to joy. His Will is eternal life for all His Children and His Will is our will.

You must trust that you all have an unmovable place in His Love. No one stands outside. There is no exception to His Universal Law of Love. You will learn to walk in your Father's Footsteps, for He has chosen well all the Children of His Love. You will take the Path now simply one step at a time, ever ascending. You will learn the lessons one day at a time.

Simply keep your eyes ever forward. Do not look to the right or to the left. Straightaway, My Brothers and Sisters! The Path we walk together is His chosen Will for all of us."

*See your self...*trusting fully in His immovable never ending love. And you as one of His Children are included forevermore in His amazing Favor.

September 22
The Focus Of Your Days

"I ask you now, again, dear Brothers and Sisters, to make loving one another the central focus of your days. Think upon these words often.

Think of anything that prevents you from loving one of your Brothers or Sisters and you will always find the root of unforgiveness as the basis for your inability to love someone.

There is such freedom in releasing any Brother or Sister from the grudges you carry. Simply take no captives.

Yes, I may seem to belabor this one particular lesson in our curriculum. But do not think this is an unnecessary lesson. It is essential."

*See your self...*releasing any, indeed, every captive you may have taken into the prison of your unforgiveness.

September 23
The Habit Of Forgiveness

"I ask you to examine your thought life periodically for the unlovely weed of unforgiveness.

You say that you have weeded carefully the gardens of your thought life, but you do discover now and then, that this particular weed has tenacious roots. Simply remove the weed again, if it should appear after its apparent removal.

The habit of unforgiveness is, indeed, deeply rooted. You need diligence. And I am here to help you. A simple reminder now and then will help to cultivate the habit of forgiveness. And one day even the weeds of the most tenacious roots will be gone and you will be totally free."

*See your self...*embracing the potential of your freedom from the habit of unforgiveness. Know that you will do all that it takes to be free from all unforgiveness.

September 24
The Power Of Choice

"You should desire freedom from negative thinking, My Brothers and Sisters. You know that negative thoughts are the weeds that crowd out the potential for spiritual fruit.

Strive daily for the removal of the weeds of unforgiveness. You do not need to carry any more burdens than those which life presents naturally. Do not add unnecessary difficulties by your own deliberate choice.

Negative thinking is *always* a choice. Negative circumstances may present great difficulty but you may choose how you handle all circumstances.

You have the power within you to release yourselves from the constant melee of negative thoughts. It is simply a habit that needs to be laid to rest. Come away with me."

See your self...daily removing all the weeds that crowd out your potential for spiritual fruit.

September 25
Depend On The Father

"It is easy to be happy when life is going your way; for indeed, you are all still very young and childlike in the handling of the difficulties on life's path. You need to trust your Father's Love and over-care more fully. You can depend on Him. His Love will carry you through as it always has thus far, even through difficulties.

Let us develop the habit together of depending on the Father to lead us. You are ready for much more of the spirit life than you realize. I eagerly await your coming away with Me. I have words always for those who have ears to hear and a ready heart to listen to the Spirit's gentle wooing."

*See your self...*as finally ready for much more of the spiritual life. You do have ears to hear and a ready heart to listen.

September 26
With Me In The Garden

"You are often the reason for the magnification of all your difficulties. You have a grave habit, developed over your lifetime. You act before you think. You need to learn to make better choices. Often this is only a matter of seeking a quiet place and learning to listen. Now, My children, you will learn to come away and sit with Me in the Garden.

Come away with Me, My beloveds. Seek eagerly these little meetings. Every one of you needs a little break now and then from your life's work and the daily stresses that life presents. Only a very few minutes is needed, habitually given over to a quiet time in My company, to bring great release to your hungry work-worn lives."

*See your self...*planning on a second meeting later in your day. "Only a very few minutes," taken away from your work-worn schedule is the requirement of this very worthy suggestion. Extra peace in your day is worth it, wouldn't you agree?

September 27
Come Into My Peace

"How many things you do each day that are really not necessary! You are angry about so much in life that you should understand is not really your concern. You trouble yourselves with world affairs while you own little world is in chaos.

Let us begin today to strive for some focus on the things in life over which you *do* have some measure of control and begin to release yourselves from that which is beyond you. Yes, you could release so many of the world's affairs.

You are surprised by this idea. Would you not come away with Me to a quiet place of stillness and rest from the affairs of state? You are Ambassadors of a heavenly Kingdom. And you are so world-weary. Let our Father take care of the world affairs. He is very capable."

See your self...removing your Self now and then from the "news" of the world's affairs and redeeming the time for more fellowship with the One Who can take care of all the insanity of the world's affairs.

September 28
The Global Front

"Release yourselves now and then from all that concerns you on the global front. Yes, there are wars and rumors of wars. But you have not a part to play in these affairs. You have a spiritual curriculum now. You have an inner kingdom to bring to peace. We will be busy in that inner kingdom in the days ahead.

Have you by all your thinking ever changed one thing at a global level? Of course not! So why go there so often?

Practice the release of those things beyond your control. It is as simple as a change of thought. Ah, again the words that your thoughts are your choice.

You choose your thoughts. You are the one who causes all the stress by a simple choice of your mental pathways. You need guidance to correct your faulty thinking. Let Me be your guide."

See your self...as a student now in a spiritual curriculum.
You can choose the direction of all your mental pathways.
Choose the positive and avoid the negative.

September 29
The Mental Realm

"To dwell in the peace that passes all understanding, you must be consistent with keeping the inner kingdom of self in control. This is the area in which you have great freedom of choice. Indeed, you have taken many wrong pathways to your places of mental captivity. You have listened to many voices that led you astray. You must turn away now from the worldly affairs that cause you fear.

Many of your Brothers and Sisters live in great fear. They are programmed by the past. I ask you today to walk a new Path with Me. Trust Me that the past is but a dream. It is not reality. You can learn to live in the present. Have faith that you and our Father can co-create a beautiful future."

> *See your self*...dwelling daily in the peace that passes all understanding. Accept that possibility as a new reality for you. You *can* co-create with our Father the most beautiful future.

September 30
The Gift Of Hope

"Allow Me to bring you the gift of hope today. Faith and hope and love are a beautiful trinity that will work for us. You may all rest assured that these three will manifest the fruits of the Spirit into your future lives.

You will find great joy in the inner kingdom as daily we labor together for a worthy life, My Brothers and Sisters. You may rest assured that it is a co-created labor that will bring abundant rewards."

> *See your self*...by the ongoing action of this "beautiful trinity," manifesting the fruits of the Spirit, now and forevermore.

OCTOBER

October 1
The Path Towards Peace

"Yes, My Beloveds, we walk on a new Path towards peace. You will learn to lay down the swords of anger and malice and you will war no more. And as each sword is laid away, you will taste the joy of freedom.

Peace is a step-by-step process. First comes the understanding. You must take personal responsibility for the simple truth that the war zones that you live in are of your own creation. With the understanding comes the possibility of victory.

You have free will and with will you have control, complete control, over the area of your thought life. So many miserable days belong now to the past, and you have the keys to the heavenly kingdom of peace and love and joy unending. Simply choose to make better choices than ever before in the inner kingdom of thought."

*See your self...*making the necessary thought adjustments to promote unending peace and love and joy throughout the remainder of your earthly journey.

October 2
Swords Of Destruction

"The habits of negative thinking are the swords of destruction that you personally wield. You can simply lay them down. Lay them down now. Choose this day to serve our Father's Will on earth. Choose to love. Only love is His Will.

If you serve as His Ambassadors, you do not carry the swords of war. You will to walk in love. You will to speak love and you will to teach love.

In laying down your swords, you *will* learn His Laws, and the kingdom of self-will will change. Slowly at first, but one day there will be only the peace on earth of His Intention. You will serve His Intention all the days of your earth existence. You want no other will and you desire no other service than His, My Brothers and Sisters.

So together we take up the cause for peace. Yes, a portion of our curriculum is cause and effect. The goal is peace on earth for all God's children."

See your self...ever aware of His goal, for all His children;
Peace on earth, and we are *all* His children.

October 3
The Goal Is Peace

"The children of every nation in Father's Universe must learn to war no more. It begins with you, My Brothers and Sisters. You must teach only love. You must personally, one by one, each and every one of you; learn the law of forgiveness.

Carry no swords of unlove. Life is much easier for those who do not bear any grudges. You must learn this lesson well Save yourselves from the captivity of unforgiveness. Lay aside this grave and very negative burden.

Let us simply take up the implements of love. Let kindness prevail in all your actions. Treat one another with gentle kindness. Return no wounds even when wounded. Learn to simply turn the other cheek.

Peace begins with those who refuse to join the battle."

*See your self...*as His child with the "love implement" of gentle kindness ever present in your daily life experiences. Love is kind and bears no grudges.

October 4
Freedom From Self Will

"You learn quickly now the curriculum of freedom. You grow stronger in the service of our Father's Will on earth. You know the rules. You aspire to peace and love. You will gain victory after victory in the battle against self will.

You know you have often, for most of your earth existence, placed your own will against Father's perfect Will, and very often self-will has robbed you of your happiness.

Now you desire only peace. You have tasted the bitterness of self-will. And you have gained glimpses of the joy attached to walking the Path in the way of truth and light.

You have gained enough understanding of His Will to know now that you must seek only love. You are the purveyors of His Will on earth. You carry the banner of Love. You are the children of Love and you are on the Path to peace."

*See your self...*daily on the Path to peace, sharing the Father's perfect Will to love one another with *everyone* you meet along this Path.

October 5
Each Path Is Unique And Perfect

"The peace that passes understanding, that peace that remains through every tribulation, is now within your reach. Understand that you are loved unconditionally. This love does not prevent the storms of life's trials. But it makes them bearable.

Eternal life is your inheritance. And while the Path is ever ascending through difficulty after difficulty, it does grow easier with each lesson learned.

You are maturing gradually in the laws of the heavenly kingdom within. You are learning the laws of love. You are taking the time to study each day with Me. I come eagerly to you as your Teacher. I know the difficulty of the Path, for I have trudged it Myself.

The difficulties of life are ever with us. Each must take the Path appointed and each must master the curriculum. Each Path is unique.

Never forget the perfection of each child's particular Path. No one is on the wrong Pathway and all are going home to Father. All of you, My Brothers and Sisters, are on the Path to Paradise. And it is totally possible for each and every one of you to stand one day in our Father's Presence. Meanwhile, simply stay grounded in the present. Trust in the perfection of Father's Plan as it unfolds.

All of you walk in His Love. Now learn to love, as He would have you love. That is always the goal of our curriculum. Teach as you learn, My children, for you are all teachers as well as students in the school of life. Ah, yes, you are both students and teachers on the Path of life and you do well, My Brothers and Sisters, in both the learning and the teaching."

*See your self...*as gaining in maturity in both learning and teaching the laws of the heavenly kingdom. Indeed, there is difficulty in the Path you have chosen, but standing one day in our Father's Presence is worth every difficulty you will master.

October 6
Teach By Example

"Yes, My beloveds, you know that I AM your Teacher and you are all My students. But I have said that "you are all teachers as well as students in the school of life."

You teach by your example. As you grow in the mastering of our curriculum, you are also teaching the curriculum. And you are presenting a better witness than you realize. You are growing quickly now in the principles of loving one another.

From time to time, the lessons are repeated, and with the repetition, the principles of the curriculum take deep roots and the weeds of self-will are loosened from your character.

You *are* becoming the children of your Father's Image, and as you grow in His Image you present a witness that teaches all the Brothers and Sisters who surround you on life's Path."

See your self growing quickly as a witness of our Father's Image. The principles are taking deep roots and the weeds of self-will are loosened daily.

October 7
Turn The Other Cheek

"The Law of forgiveness, quickly practiced, is the incredible witness of your growth. You are learning now to "turn the other cheek" and to forgive without bearing a single grudge. You are quick to abandon the burden of unforgiveness, and indeed, you are learning to leave its tenacious weeds behind. The past is no longer a detriment to your future."

See your self burden free walking daily in the Father's Perfect forgiveness Law.

October 8
Live In The Present

"The kingdom of heaven is now established in the lives of our Father's Children, in those who are aware of His curriculum and who gladly take the lessons presented each day in the full knowledge that His Will is perfect and His curriculum is faultless.

There is no need to hurry on the Path, My Beloveds. I want you to disregard any sense of urgency to complete the curriculum. Father's Plan for your steady advancement is perfect. No need for a sense of failure either because you do not quickly learn the lessons presented. Often you learn by trial and error. And you know that this is the truth.

You have cried out, "How often must I fail?" And I say to you, "Be patient!" You hear Me tell you often that you do well on the journey. Trust Me also in this beautiful truth. You are advancing step by step towards the goal of peace on earth. And I have told you that it begins with you. There is enough to do each day without ever taking any burdens of unforgiveness from the day before."

*See your self...*forgiving your Self for a lack of patience with your Self. The journey provides everything you need and you are progressing beautifully.

October 9
Wounded In Battle

"Peace *will* come, My beloveds, for that is our Father's Will. And it is your desire that His Will becomes a reality. Peace is slow in coming. The centuries pass by and His Universal Law to love one another is not universally practiced. But you, My Brothers and Sisters, understand there is no other way for peace on Earth except that all mankind practice forgiveness.

If you have been wounded on any battleground from a previous day, I ask you to heal yourself, Release you own wounds to the healing balm of forgiveness. And yes, you wound yourselves far too often.

And forgive yourselves for you own impatience with the journey. The Path is perfect! I will remind you often of this truth."

See your self...fully accepting the perfection of the Path. Release all who have wounded you along the Path with the gift of total forgiveness thus receiving self-healing as the gift you give your Self.

October 10
Walk In His Will

"You are propagating His Will on earth. And if there are difficult days ahead as you put His Laws into practice, you will surmount the difficulties because you love Him and hunger deeply for His Will on earth.

We study His curriculum together. It never changes. It is the same, yesterday, today and forever. Until you learn to forgive, you cannot walk in His Will."

See your self...as a student of His curriculum, walking daily in His Will because you love Him with all your heart, mind, and strength.

October 11
Peace Begins With You

"Walking in our Father's Will each day, My Beloveds, is the Path to peace. His Will is often greatly confused with mankind's will. An eye for an eye is not our Father's Will, although many of Our Father's children believe in this false doctrine. They live their entire lives believing that every wound demands a like wound. No! This is man's law not God's. You must forgive one another every wound.

And although you may sometimes think that mankind may never come to peace, and that all wars may never cease, I tell you this truth today; peace begins with you.

You can bring peace to the little world that surrounds you. You can learn to lay down your personal swords. I would have you become gardeners in our Father's Universe and not be soldiers of war."

See your self...as a gardener in our Father's beautiful Universe, beating every sword of war into a plowshare of peace.

October 12
Rumors Of War

"I know there are rumors of war. But I ask you today to take courage in Father's Love. His Plans go far beyond what is seen in the physical world. Fear Not! Father is not impotent in the office to champion His Universal Will.

Understand always that you are not alone and that good will always prevail; contrary to the thinking of the doomsayers. Fear not! Father has no intention beyond Love. And you can rest well in the assuredness that this Universe will endure."

See your self...never numbered among the warmongers or doomsayers. Understand always that good *will* prevail, for He causes ALL things to work for the good.

October 13
Words Of Encouragement

"Yes, My beloveds, in these troubled times, I seek to reward your diligence in attending our meetings with words of encouragement. Things around you are unsettling. Rumors are filling your minds with fearful thoughts. But I tell you the truth. You need not fear the future. You are building a future in the present.

Take this day as the beautiful gift you have received. Return the Love of our Father that you are receiving and give it away this day. You do not need to listen to the words of the fear mongers. Your can choose to lay aside the fears. I AM with you. You are unconditionally loved and you can take Our Father's Love abroad today.

You can take the sunshine of His Love everywhere you step. And you can choose to think on the love of God and the ways in each day that are given to you to share this love. Many opportunities will arise today for the little loving actions of kindness. Choose wisely."

See your self..wisely choosing to extend our Father's Love to all that you encounter along the Path each day.

October 14
Through The Storms

"You can do much to bring peace today by walking fearlessly forward through the storms of life. You have come though many fearful storms before and you will survive the present ones, too. Keep your eyes on what is good and, by choice, remove your thinking from the negative."

See your self..walking fearlessly forward. You can do this, for you *can* do ALL things through Christ Who strengthens you.

October 15
An Environment Of Peace

"We have spoken before of the smile on your face and the gentle touch. And you can speak words of peace. You know how to curb the tongue's angry words. You need not wound another Brother or Sister with any thoughtless words. Think before you speak.

And when you put away the swords of anger you still the wars within, and peace on earth becomes a reality.

You can make a difference. You are Father's Ambassadors of Love. You can speak His Love abroad. And person-by-person through the ministrations of every child in His Service, the love command is carried to every Brother and Sister in His Universe. We go *together* each day, walking in the curriculum of truth to change the world. The goal is *always* peace. And you are the peacemakers.

Live in love, and peace will come. Yes, it is our Father's Will that peace will come to every child in His Universe. You must do your part, each and every one of you, My Brother's and Sisters. You must personally carry the Father's Will to love one another to each and every Brother and Sister that you meet along life's Path."

See your self...making a difference in the lives of your Brothers and Sisters. You are His peacemakers and the ministers of His glorious command to love one another as He does love each and every one of us.

October 16
Who Is My Neighbor?

"You must leave no one standing outside the arms of love. You can be the administrator of our Father's Gospel of Love. You can make a difference in some unloved person's life this very day. You can focus your attention on the Father's love commandment; love your neighbor.

You may ask, "Who is my neighbor?" You are *all* neighbors. The only distance between your neighborhoods are the boundaries of your unforgiveness. Create no boundaries. Father's Love encompasses all who live within His Universe."

*See your self...*fully accepting His Vision that all His children are, indeed, your neighbors and all worthy as His children for the extension of your love.

October 17
Citizens Of The Universe

"He calls you to become citizens of all He has created. Expand your horizons today. You owe no allegiance to any bounded country. You are His Children and the Servants of His Will on earth. And if I tell you that wherever you place your foot in whatever your extended circumstances, and to whatever galaxy or galaxies you may ascend, you will only have one service to His Will.

For all eternity you will be in the service to the curriculum of love. Listen to My Words. And learn this one truth well. Owe no one anything except the debt of all your love for all the days of your existence. And the days of your existence are without number."

*See your self...*devoted to the Father's Will to love one another.

October 18
Servants Of Love

"I call you this day, My beloveds, to the service of Love. You will answer that call. You will never need to answer any other call to service but this one, for indeed; love should encompass every service you offer.

In this new day you will receive many opportunities to love one another. I ask you to administer love as the antidote to any semblance of ill will.

I told you once, that our Father delights in the happiness of His children. Would you not choose this day to bring happiness to our Father's day? Has He not so often brought happiness to you?

You must love one another and practice forgiveness. You must leave the battles of life to our Father. There is no need for unnecessary warfare.

Give the gift of love today to all you meet. Consistently make the choice that is our Father's Will for all His children. Love one another. Serve one another."

*See your self...*in His Service to love all your Brothers and Sisters.

October 19
I Am Your Friend

"I am your Friend and I am here with you now. I delight in our daily meetings, and so do you. You can see evidence of progress on the Path. You are growing in patience, especially with yourselves. You are far less critical of one another. You are beginning to see, as our Father would have you see.

Simply continue to come to Me each day. I have good council to offer you. Learn this lesson well, My Brothers and Sisters. You are loved. You are love. Learn to give as you have boundlessly received."

*See your self...*as a minister in His Love Service. Yes, and give as you have, indeed, "boundlessly received."

October 20
Offer Assistance

"You understand that many of your Brothers and Sisters are not meeting daily with Me. Many are on the Path with little assistance of which they are aware. Many stumble and fall.

You, however, are learning to offer assistance when you can. You are learning the value of a smile or an unexpected kindness. Love is growing in your own life and is extending outward now to all that surrounds you. You are conscious now of the good that you are able to cast about you. And the ministry of love will grow until one day it will encompass the entire world.

You cannot stifle the growth of love. In all its magnificence it will heal every wound and remove all pain and suffering.

Be happy for this day and for another opportunity to spread our Father's Love and offer its healing balm to all you meet."

*See your self...*truly as a minister of our Father's Will to love one another. Applaud your Self this very day for your diligence to spread the Love of God abroad.

October 21
Persist On The Path

"You must persist, My Brothers and Sisters, in the laws of our Father's Will on earth. You are responsible for what you think and you can choose to clothe yourselves in the garment of a happy thought life as opposed to the choice of unruly thinking.

Stop finding fault with one another and begin to see one another through Father's Eyes. See with His Understanding. See with Vision. You must overlook the faults and give one another credit for how far each of you have actually come in all the negativity that befalls each and every one of you.

You have come far through many trials and great tribulations and so has each of your Brothers and Sisters. Learn to see as Father sees.

Learn this lesson well. You are all in the curriculum of life. And many have had higher mountains to climb and deeper, far more difficult crosses to bear than you could ever comprehend. You must add no additional heavy burden to another Brother or Sister.

Be careful of the words you speak. Think carefully on the matter of the idle words that injure. You must speak only love. You have a task before you now to monitor your tongue. Check your thinking and be sure you injure no one with your senseless idle chatter."

*See your self...*learning to control your tongue. The practice of thinking before you speak will lead you to the mastery of your tongue, so necessary in the victory over the idle words that injure.

October 22
Walk In His Image

"I call you to a deeper walk now as Father's Ambassadors. I call you now to a more thoughtful and kinder service than ever before. I call you to arise to a higher place in the kingdom within and guard against all unloving thoughts or actions.

Walk in His Image *now*! You can do this for I go with you. I take your hand each day as we walk this Path together.

I know that often you feel alone. You are *never* alone. And when you feel abandoned, it is simply an unruly emotion. You can choose to believe the truth, or allow your unruly emotions to rule the inner kingdom.

Many of you create your own hells on earth in your undisciplined thought life. Come with Me. I will bring you to Peace."

*See your self...*releasing your Self from many of the hells of your own making. You can choose the truth and rule your inner kingdom by releasing all your unruly emotions. Be patient. You can do this or He wouldn't ask you to try.

October 23
Trials And Tribulations

"Trials and tribulations are *always* to be expected on the Path we travel. You must learn the simple acceptance of the trials. Life is all about growth. You cannot stand still. You must evolve and you must learn to climb higher even with the adversity you encounter. Just accept that the trials are a part of the curriculum.

Trials never change one truth that you must learn. I am *always* with you. Listen to My words. Trust Me fully. I have said that trials will come and we can walk through any trial together. And you will see victory on every one of the battlefields of life.

You grow stronger each day, and yes, you grow stronger in trust. We will see every trial through to victory. Never forget you are Father's Ambassadors of love, and love is *always* victorious."

*See your self...*determined to remember this one great truth. Our Beloved Master and Teacher is *always* with us.

October 24
Accomplishment

"It is another beautiful day. Perhaps the prospect of this day is not very exciting. You have ordinary chores to accomplish. And perhaps you grow weary sometimes of the ordinary days. You cannot have days of constant excitement or pleasure. There is always the business of the daily chores. But you should be happy for the ordinary days.

Even so, there are exciting days ahead on the Path we tread together. Are you aware of how quickly this month passes? Are you conscious of the acceleration of time? Yet, you have come far in just a very short time. We have accomplished much."

*See your self...*happy in the ordinary days. Our Father expects this from all His children. Perhaps something we should accomplish in our life experience is the simplicity of happiness in the ordinary days.

October 25
Encouragement

"Let Me encourage you today to simply trust our Father's Curriculum! It is perfect! The days ahead have our lessons in perfect order, planned to give you the growth necessary for the completion of your personal part in the growth of our Father's Kingdom. You have work to accomplish and even the very ordinary days are very much a part of His Plan.

Enjoy this day. Receive its gift and its purpose in your heart and do *all* you can to accomplish our Father's Perfect Will.

Love all your Brothers and Sisters. And walk this day in perfect confidence, My Beloveds, that you walk on a Path of His Choice for each and every one of you."

*See your self...*accepting with gratitude the gift of this beautiful day, and acknowledge with full acceptance the perfection of your Path.

October 26
The Father's Love

"Yes, My beloveds, you most certainly walk on the Path of Father's Choice. No one is on the Path apart from our Father's knowing. All walk within His loving Embrace. *ALL* are loved unconditionally. We have touched on this subject briefly before. But it is time for a little review.

Father places no conditions on His Love. There is nothing you can do to gain His Love. You already possess it fully. He does not love you on some days and forget to love you on others. Please remember that there is absolutely nothing you can do to gain His Love or to lose it. His Love simply is."

*See your self...*accepting fully, in all its simplicity, the amazing fact that Father loves you unconditionally and He always will.

October 27
Unconditional Love

"Unconditional love is a hard lesson for some of you to understand, for all of you have been loved conditionally and have learned to love others conditionally as a result. Life is, after all, about cause and effect. You can stop this negative cycle by simply accepting the Father's Love.

He gives love freely to all His Children and you are *all* His Children. He asks for nothing as a price for His Love. There is no charge! Freely have you received; freely give.

Give His Love away, unconditionally, as you seek to follow consistently in His Image."

*See your self...*receiving Father's unconditional Love as the Highest of His great blessings. And step eagerly into this day prepared to love *all* who share this Path with you.

October 28
Perfectly Loveable

"You will learn to love the "unloveable" for it is you who have placed this title upon some of your Brothers and Sisters. If our all knowing and all loving Father envisions *all* of you as perfectly loveable, then surely you can learn to do the same.

If you know someone whom you cannot love, then you know a place to begin the new learning process. Release that brother or sister to the simple understanding that Father loves them and so can you.

There is none who stands outside the loving embrace of our Father. And in time, our lessons will teach you all to leave no one standing outside of our loving embrace.

Rule the kingdom of heaven that is within you by carefully removing that which poisons, and replacing the poisons with thoughts of love."

See your self...embracing this very day the heavenly kingdom rule of non-judgment. It would not be asked of you, if you could not do it.

October 29
Perfectly Understandable

"There is good in all your religious philosophies. However, you must learn one very important fact. The Father's Love is *not* earned by what your religions teach you.

Your religions are your choice for living in your society. Pick the one that gives you personal happiness, one that you find perfectly understandable for you. And allow all your Brothers and Sisters to make their own personal choice in the matter.

The freedom of choice is Father's Will for *all* His Children. Judge not another's standards. Take the time you waste in judgment and put it to better use. Use that time to raise your own standards higher."

See your self...redeeming the time wasted on criticism and judgment. Giving up all criticism and judgment immediately raises your own standards higher.

October 30
Religious Judgment

"We talked briefly yesterday of the personal choice that each of you make in the religion that you follow. And some of you have chosen to follow no religious philosophy at all. In either case, I have asked you not to judge one another's standard of faith.

You will see that non-judgment is a kingdom rule for your personal freedom. Do not judge another's standard of religion or politics. Simply refrain from judgment. For in truth, your judgment will not change their thinking one iota.

If the Father's Desire is that you waste no time in your foolish judgments, you can see that the time saved can be put to a better use."

*See your self...*wasting no more of our precious time in "foolish" judgments. Enough said!

October 31
Thought Adjustment

"Kingdom living is possible by simply breaking a few habits and establishing a few others. The few minutes that we spend together each day will put you on a Path of well-adjusted thinking. You are learning now some very valuable thinking principles.

I have shown you the areas that have needed some mental adjustments.

Unforgiveness is a waste of our valuable time.

Bearing grudges has no value whatsoever.

Anger is fruitless and potentially destructive.

Let Me lead you away from the nonsense of your endless supply of the bad seeds of negative thinking. Let us build some new and better habits."

*See your self...*working daily on the Path of "well-adjusted thinking." Allow our older Wiser Brother to lead you daily in building new and better habits.

NOVEMBER

November 1
Set Aside Criticism

"Set aside criticism. I ask what purpose is truly served by criticizing another Brother or Sister's choice on the Path? None whatsoever! You cannot change the path they choose. Each must follow the directions of their own heads and hearts. You must allow them all to make their own choices.

Like you, they will make many poor choices in judgment. But are any choices really poor or actually unwise? Not really, for in the errors you make, you learn what not to do again.

From the errors you learn to make a better choice. And a better future depends on the lessons well learned and the better choices continually made."

*See your self...*with enhanced focus on better choices.
Slow down, as this is a key to a better future.

November 2
Lay Aside Judgment

"Lay all judgment aside. You are all on the Path at different levels of growth. You are each evolving consistently to a higher level. You are asked to only offer assistance when you can, and lay no stumbling block in the Path of any Brother or Sister.

Your judgments are never truly honest, for you never truly know all the details. You are only surface judging.

Our Father, however, knows all the details and He will guide the steps in full understanding of every footfall that each of His Children takes.

Let Father direct the Pathways. You must concern yourselves with your own personal curriculum each day. There is enough to keep us all very busy."

See your self...following these very wise directions. Concern your Self with no other Pathway but your own.

November 3
Doubts And Worries

"I ask you today, My Brothers and Sisters, to lay aside all doubts and worries. There is nothing to fear. I AM with you always. You can depend on our loving relationship.

I AM with you in the stillness and also in the troubled chaos of some of your days. You can know peace in every situation as you learn to fully trust in My unfailing Presence.

We have quite a distance to travel together. For in every moment of your future I AM with you and the future is truly endless. Trust fully in My never-ending love. I care for you like no other can ever care.

These words are truth and they should bring you great joy and happiness. Depend fully on Me."

See your self...depending fully on the Presence of His never failing love, a love like no other.

November 4
Put Aside Anger

"Put aside all anger. It is counter-productive. It is a senseless emotion for the most part. It rarely serves our Father's Purpose. Anger is useless. It is a waste of time. Seeding Love, however, reaps a bountiful harvest.

You wonder at the phrase "righteous anger." When is anger ever useful? It is easier to ask the question, when is it counter productive? If it is a useless emotion, then put it away. When it will harm another Brother or Sister, it is ungodly.

Always ask these questions. What will anger do in this situation that will create good? What will this anger accomplish? Rarely will anger accomplish any good at all. And it can be both harmful to you as well as to your Brothers and Sisters."

*See your self...*working daily to remove the useless *habit* of anger from your curriculum.

November 5
Disconnect Impatience

"You will find, My Beloveds, that anger is a weed with deep roots. I ask you now to learn to control your anger. See how often in this very day you will have opportunities to break this habit of long standing.

Anger is the sister weed to impatience. Yes, you know this is a great truth. Anger is an unpleasant character trait that has caused you to feel some distaste in your character growth. Yet, you would have patience.

I have given you a key to finding patience, for patience grows slowly in your evolutionary process, but the path to patience is the release of anger. How easy it is now, with these few simple statements, to realize the control of anger bears the fruit of patience."

*See your self...*growing in patience every time you release the weed of anger from the garden of your life experience.

November 6
Control Your Emotions

"Yes, My Brothers and Sisters, you will see fruit when you sow the seeds of love. Be consistent! Daily take your ready smile to all you meet. And be kind to one another. Sow the seeds of kindness and then see the gentle blossoms of your kindness returned.

You are our Father's Children and you must walk the Path in His Will. Love is His Will and He desires that you serve His Law of Love.

Learn to control your emotions. They are so often simply habits acquired as children. Lay them aside like a worn out useless garment. You must shed the love of God in every corner of this universe."

*See your self...*dressing your Self each day in the garment of our Father's Love. And yes, *see your Self,* laying aside the useless garments of emotions run rampant.

November 7
Do Not Be Discouraged

"Be not discouraged, My Children, when you discover you are fallible. You will find these negative weeds deeply rooted. You are human! But I would never direct your path to the impossible.

You are intelligent children and you can get the weeding accomplished easily when you understand the principle. You need to simply reason the principle through.

The gardening process is ongoing. Daily you *will* labor in your mental gardens. Be consistent.

You will see the gardens of your thought life vastly improved in a very short period of time; just with the understanding of these principles of law in the kingdom of our Father's universal Will.

Do not be discouraged, My Brothers and Sisters, with the deep-rooted weeds in your mental gardens. You have come far."

See your self...doing the mental weeding that is required each day. Every negative thought you remove allows space for the blossoms from every positive seed you plant.

November 8
Perpetual Students

"Now a new day is before us. We face its challenges knowing there is *great perfection* in the curriculum of life. If you trust that the curriculum is perfect, then you can embrace the future with great happiness. You are after all, My Brothers and Sisters, *perpetual* students.

The days ahead are truly a great adventure when you simply trust the perfection of the Path. The days pass quickly. If you could more fully trust My Words, the ordinary days that lead ever forward would give you, oh so much more pleasure.

Enjoy today! It's a very important day in our Father's grand Plan. For indeed, every day is a holy part of His Perfection."

See your self...Fully trusting in the perfection of the Path, for indeed trust will give you so much more pleasure even in the ordinary days.

November 9
Servants To Peace

"There are rumors of war. These are troublesome days for many. You must be servants to peace. Every time there is an opportunity to take the path of peace and resist the path of war, you know the choice you must make.

You are children of His Kingdom of Love. You are called as peacemakers. Serve only in His Service, and the days will stretch forth before you in joy and peace. No matter what the rumors may be, you may live in peace in the chaos, My Beloveds, and that is the peace that passes all understanding."

*See you self...*as His servants in His Kingdom of Love, ever ready to establish His Peace in the chaos.

November 10
Allegiance To God

"I have much to say to you this day, My Brothers and Sisters. There can, indeed, be peace in the chaos. Though nations may crumble around you, you know Whose children you are. You are the children of our Father's Kingdom. You owe no true allegiance to any other kingdom but His.

You may live in a country and you may follow the leadings of your country's leaders. However, they are the heads of paper governments. You are called to serve Father's Will. You cannot let the leaders take away your peace.

You have a choice to make *each* day. Choose to follow our Father's Law to love one another."

*See your self...*realizing, perhaps for the very first time, that if we were to truly love one another, as is the Father's Perfect Will, there is never any need for war fare of any kind for any reason.

November 11
Freedom Of Choice

"Indeed, you live in very chaotic time. You do not need to agree with those who refuse the commands to love one another. Nonetheless, it is possible to disagree in your minds and your hearts without throwing any stones.

You can refuse to follow the insanity of those who refuse our Father's Will. You are totally free in your minds. Choose this day to cast no stones, none whatsoever, particularly in the mental realm.

I have often talked to you of the freedom of choice. Choose to remain free. Nations may crumble. They may choose the path of war. But it need not be your choice. But again I say, My Beloveds, give our Father your true allegiance.

Remain in the inner Kingdom. The Heavenly Kingdom within need never know the chaos from without. You are the rulers of your mental kingdoms. And you have only our Father's Will to serve there. He knows, oh so well, those who choose to serve His inner Kingdom of Perfect Peace.

My Beloveds, choose today to wholeheartedly serve our Father in His Will to love one another. There is no need to live in the chaos of the world. I have said that while you live in the world, you need not live in its chaos.

You have chosen a way to live now that calls you to the service of love. You have listened to My Words. You know the Path to Peace. You will simply lay aside the implements of war. These are not physical implements. You will simply train your minds to know war no more."

See your self...understanding the mental chaos that you create so often for your Self. You can train your Self to follow always a mental path to peace.

November 12
Do Unto Others

"As you go about your chores today, My Brothers and Sisters, remember that you are Our Father's Children. Treat each other with *great* kindness.

'Do unto others, as you would have them do unto you.' Yes, these words have echoed through the centuries. Yet, the Golden Rule is often forgotten. How wonderful it is to learn this rule and practice its wisdom each and every day."

See your self...not as one who has forgotten the Golden Rule. Yes, practice its wisdom continually and bring great delight to our Father, the Source of *all* good.

November 13
The Good Life

"It has been said in the scriptures; " Choose this day Whom you will serve." These words, too, echo through the centuries. Choose to serve our Father's Will. Choose to love and forgive whenever and wherever these choices arise.

Today you have choices to make. Would you serve our Father's Will on earth? Would you love one another, as He would have you love?

You will have opportunities today to choose to serve Him or to serve self-will. It must be your choice for the good life, My Brothers and Sisters. And indeed, the good life is earned through the good choices that you make each day. Choose this day to serve Father's universal Law to love one another."

*See your self...*fully in alignment with our Father's Will. Practice daily His universal Law of Love for all His children universally.

November 14
The Quiet Place

"There is a quiet place in your mind where we can meet. I AM *always* there.

Yes, My Beloveds, I AM your Friend. I AM always with you. Nothing will ever change that. There is no friendship like this nor can there ever be. In the stillness of your mind I dwell.

But you can take me into the chaos also. For Indeed, I take your hand *each* day. *Always* we move forward together.

I have told you these words before. Why do I repeat them? Because, dear Brothers and Sisters, you do forget that you are *never* alone. You resist this great truth. You do forget in the difficulties that I AM always with you and that you face *nothing whatsoever* by yourself.

Still your mind and listen."

*See your self...*learning to still your mind to listen, especially in the chaos situations that life so often presents.

November 15
Stilling Your Mind

"You must learn the importance of stilling mind. This is not an easy task. Trust that My Voice is but an instant away from your hearing. However, you do not need to sit quietly or learn some form or practice that summons Me to your side. There is no special prayer that brings Me to you.

Learning to still your mind takes but an instant in time with purpose. And in that instant you and I and Father will meet together.

We delight with your determined, wholehearted intention to meet with us."

*See your self...*with a determined effort to do so, creating a meeting place with our older, wiser Brother, and Our Father, the Father of the Universe. Quite a Trinity wouldn't you say?

November 16
In God's Presence

"I have said, "Call on Me and I *will* answer." You must make the call!

Stilling your mind is a simple as saying, "Come to me." You may use whatever words come to mind. You say a simple hello in greeting your friends. You may say, "Hello Father, I am here." And you are in our Presence in that instant that you call the attention of your awareness to our Presence. The Presence is always with you. It is your attention that needs that training.

Let it suffice for today that you fully understand that the eternal Presence is *always* present. You will call and we will be there in the stillness of that holy instant. And you *will* learn to trust completely in this truth."

*See your self...*with a growing desire for more trust in this perfect curriculum. Trust fully in the Presence of this magnificent Trio that you are in partnership with.

November 17
You And I Are One

"As you read My Words now, My Beloveds, know that I AM with you in this classroom of our intent.

I have said, "I and My Father are one." Understand these words as a call to unity. There is never any separation between us. We are of one Mind and one Will. And you and I are one. We are *never* separate from one another. Nor can you ever be separated from our Father.

You are learning to separate yourself from self-will. You are learning to follow the Father's Will and His alone."

*See your self...*reading these words with the full understanding that you are in humanity's classroom in complete unity with the Will of our Father to continually love one another.

November 18
Through Father's Eyes

"You can learn to see yourselves through our Father's Eyes. He would have you see each other through His Eyes also.

If He remembers none of your failures or errors, and you would learn to follow His Will, then quickly learn to forgive. And also learn to forget all the grievances. Carry no burden from one day into another. Walk the Path in total freedom. The past can be an incredible burden to carry.

You already know this truth. But we will review this universal principle often. Learn to be merciful, as Father is merciful. And learn to understand fully the freedom that lies in forgiving and forgetting. Forgiveness is the Path to Freedom."

*See your self...*learning to be merciful. It is a major part of the curriculum. You can do it!

November 19
Relax And Trust

"Your days would be far more pleasant for you if you would simply relax and trust that the curriculum is truly perfect. Trust will grow as you see yourself making better choices.

You are learning to love, as Our Father would have you love, and I would ask you today this question. Are you not a better Lover of the Brothers and Sisters who surround you today than you were just a short time ago? Yes, of course you are! This is proof that His curriculum is working!

The universe is evolving towards Love, divine Love. It may seemingly take eons of time if measured by your impatience. So why not learn to relax more, and simply trust Father's Will in the Perfection that it is?"

*See your self...*fully accepting this very day that the curriculum *is* working. Yes, accept, allow and surrender to the perfection of our Father's Plan.

November 20
The Better Way

"I have told you before that you can choose the better way. Sometimes this is difficult, for you have not gained full emotional maturity. Maturity is not an age; it is a developing portion of your evolution.

Be patient. Simply take one step at a time. You are moving forward.

You are getting stronger. You must understand that the habits of a lifetime die slowly.

Now, for today, what can you do to bring happiness and peace into this day? Simply live it to its fullest. You are asked to give love whenever the call to love arrives and it will arrive, My Brothers and Sisters. It is a simple kindness that tells the world you know you are your Father's Child."

*See your self...*searching for every opportunity to extend the Father's Love to everyone you meet on the Path today. It is the Father's Love command that we serve always as His most beloved Children.

November 21
Learn The Truth

"His curriculum is truth. You must learn the truth. You are here in this flesh existence to learn the Will of our Father and to teach these lessons as you learn them. Yes, you are both students and teachers in the curriculum of love.

You are good students and also good teachers. You learn quickly. You desire unity. You have discovered Whose children you are, and with each passing day, you realize more fully the value of the curriculum.

You desire only the peace that comes from following the Father's Will and only His Will for the extension of His amazing Love to all. You are the Lovers that He sends to represent His Image."

*See your self...*as the Lover our Father uses to extend His "amazing" Love to all.

November 22
Channels Of His Peace

"Yes, My Beloveds, you are all here to represent our Father's Love. You are here on behalf of His Will on earth. You are all individual channels of His Peace and Love. Yet, as you know, you sometimes fall short of your potential. You do not always love, as our Father would have you love. Why? You are so often the victim of your own emotions.

You do not have total victory in the emotional realm for you are both students and teachers in the curriculum of our Father's Will on earth. You teach by your example. You are becoming the disciples of His Image. You *will* show forth His Goodness as you travel the Path."

> *See your self*...seeking victory in the emotional realm.
> Loving *all* your Brothers and Sisters, even though there
> may be those who seem unlovable to you.

November 23
Count Your Blessings

"My Beloved Brothers and Sisters, do you need to be reminded today to be kind to one another and to smile often? If no, then simply go about your day with the sunshine of a happy attitude. If however, your mood is not happy, then you may definitely need an attitude adjustment.

Many of your Brothers and Sisters walk their paths today with far heavier burdens to bear than yours. You would do well to simply return your thinking to the simple process of counting your blessings, for surely there are many."

> *See your self*...taking a few minutes to review your
> blessings. Count them one by one, perhaps even writing
> them down; for surely there are very many, indeed.

November 24
Return To Love

"You are on a Path to return to Love. I will guide you daily in these lessons, today, tomorrow and forever. You will learn to love, as our Father would have you love. You will learn to love as our Father loves. You will learn to love unconditionally the entire family of God without reservation.

Let us walk the Path in joy and happiness, My Brothers and Sisters. Why not continue onward as Father would have us continue? A good day lies before us. Let us walk it as He would have us walk it, with peace in our hearts and smiles on our faces."

*See your self...*as a most willing student of our Father's Will to love all others as He loves us. Learning this lesson will turn even the emotionally cloudy days into days of amazing brilliance.

November 25
The Insignia of Love

"My Brothers and Sisters, I have told you that your smile is the insignia of love. And I have asked you to smile often. It is a kind act and so easy to perform. It can bring happiness in an instant. Smile often today. Have you not ever looked in the mirror and studied your smile? It brings beauty to your face in an instant.

Children smile easily. You have seen a child play quietly and alone with a happy smile upon its face. And, indeed, you have seen beauty in that smile. As Father's Children, you will learn to give this beautiful gift to all you meet.

Understand it as a loving service. Understand it as the insignia of our Father's Service as you serve His Will on earth. And simply go about your day prepared to give this love signal often."

See your self...smiling more frequently. The "Insignia of Love" is a visible sign you can offer to all you meet upon the Path today and every day. It's a great and very creative habit you can so easily adopt to your growing godly character.

November 26
Growing In Wisdom

"You are happier than you realize. You are unafraid of the future. You are learning to walk the Path in His Love. And you are prepared to take each day as it comes, ready for all the perfect lessons.

You have had some mental victories. There have been places in your thinking where the choice was made for peace. You know the inner Kingdom may indeed, be either the Heaven or hell of your personal choosing.

You are growing daily in wisdom and you will continue to grow in this new wisdom, My Brothers and Sisters, as we walk the Path. The days of peace will become more frequent as you fully come to understand your responsibility to the peace that passes understanding."

See your self...doing all that is required to establish the heavenly Kingdom within. You can choose Heaven or hell. And you certainly know your preference for Heaven is the same as our Heavenly Father's choice for you.

November 27
We Are One Family

"Indeed, we are one family, My Brothers and Sisters. We are bonded together in an unbreakable relationship. This will *never* change. Emotions may change your feelings about this inseparable bond, but reality is not changed.

You may think of yourself as separate one from another, but this is not the truth. There is only unity in our Father's Family. There is only love in the Spirit. The Father delights in your growth. You become more like Him with every passing day."

*See your self…*growing daily in the Love curriculum and becoming more like our Father with every passing day.

November 28
I Will Give You Rest

"You concentrate so intently on the daily chores of life that you forget your need to come away with Me now and then. You need the refreshment and comfort of little breaks from the daily tasks both mental and physical.

No one is capable of constant weeding. There is no need for constant busyness. Rest often from the mental chores. Diligence and persistence at the weeding is necessary, but not to the point of exhaustion. Come away with Me for a few moments from your labors on the Path and I will give you rest."

See your self… embracing His suggestion for restoration when you come away daily with our Beloved Friend for these few precious moments.

November 29
All The Help You Need

"Rest in this truth. I have told you "one step at a time" is how we go, and that we go together hand in hand along the Path. You *will* receive all the help you need.

Stand tall in the knowledge that you are loved. You are loved completely. And you are provided for. This knowledge is truth. You have sought love and all the while you had it.

You know now you are always home in Father's Arms. And you can *never* move beyond His Love. Be patient with His Path for you. There is no need to hurry.

And learning to take little rests with Me will make the journey far more pleasant. Stop along your Path each day for just a few minutes now and then. I am always ready to stop with you, to hold you in My Arms and soothe your troubled brow.

Rest assured, yes, with great confidence in My constant Presence with you. You are *never* alone."

*See your self...*taking some little rest stops along the Path each day. Yes, rest assured in His ever- present immeasurable Love for you.

November 30
There Is Much To Learn

"Learning to still your mind takes but an instant in time with purpose. And in that instant you and I and Father will meet together. We delight with your determined, wholehearted intention to meet with us.

You come eagerly now to our morning meetings and you are seeking the little quiet times in each day. You are learning the value of a balanced life. Work, play and rest are all the important ingredients to your continual growth in your evolutionary progress.

You know that we can meet in the quiet times for rest and refreshment together. And I will tell you now that you bring our Father much delight with your discipline and persistence in the Kingdom principles.

There is much to learn, My Brothers and Sisters, and the learning makes our adventure very exciting. You are growing daily into His Perfect Image. And you are finding some delight now and then in your progress. You have more moments of actual joy and you do find more pleasure in your daily accomplishments.

We have come far together in these past few months. Let us continue in the curriculum that our Father places in our Path each day. Trust in the perfection of His Plan for each and every one of your precious lives. He is with us in every moment and we delight to accompany you on this journey in the daily adventure in Kingdom living."

See your self...trusting in the perfection of Father's Perfect Plan that leads us ever onward toward His goal for the peace that passes all understanding.

DECEMBER

December 1
Lean On Me

"I AM always with you, My Brothers and Sisters. We are moving steadily forward into a very interesting month. And it is a month of great accomplishment!

You are good students. You give your best to every day. And I tell you now that we are very pleased with the steady progress of each of our students.

You need not worry about the days ahead. Look forward with confidence that we will continue on a path of great accomplishment. We go hand in hand each day as I have told you before. Lean on me.

I call you now to a new level of emotional responsibility, for you are ready to grow in this area. Controlling your emotions is a *very* important part of our curriculum together."

See your self...as His "good student," giving daily thought to your present responsibility for growth in the control of your emotions.

December 2
A Great Adventure

"Yes, My Brothers and Sisters, life is a great adventure. Each day is a little adventure in itself. From moment to moment the Path of your particular journey unfolds. And in truth, each path is a totally unique experience.

You all face an original future with no two paths being the same. You are all telling a story and no story is like another's.

You have days of trials and days that cause you pain. This is all necessary to the growth of your character.

You need to experience all the emotions, both those that bring you happiness and those that create sadness, too.

You must experience the mountain top emotions as well as the deep valleys of pain and suffering.

This is all part of the earth experience. Remember *always* that you are *never* alone in the highs and lows of your emotions. I AM with you."

See your self... in every experience coupled with the great I AM. You are **never** alone. And thus will it ever be.

December 3
Emotions Come And Go

"A part of the journey's lesson is that you learn to live in the emotions without allowing the emotions to consume your thinking. Emotions come and go, and you can learn to control them, and not allow them to rule your thought life.

The happy emotions are not the problem. No! You can enjoy them. But accept that they are only temporary.

And when you experience those emotions that appear debilitating, accept also that they are temporary, too."

See your self...growing daily in emotional maturity. You are making consistent headway in the curriculum.

December 4
Emotional Fluctuation

"My Beloveds, emotions come and go like the tides at the seashore. Especially vulnerable are you during holidays, for you are always subject to emotional fluctuations.

Some days you are very happy. You know accomplishment. You know that I AM with you. You arise and face the day with great expectation. Yet with all your faith, you arise some days with doubts and emotional turmoil.

On these days you wonder why you are fearful. Where did your faith go? What has happened to your courage? Why do you feel discouraged on some days and not on others?

Let Me say this – and try to understand My Words – If you can control your thinking, ... and you know you can, ... then you can control your emotions. You can change the way you feel about anything in any moment."

See your self...on the days when you *feel* fearful or discouraged and perhaps with your faith stockpile at its lowest ebb, you can change it all in an instant by adjusting your thinking to God's perspective. You are totally in control of your thinking.

December 5
Childish Thinking

"Yes, My Brothers and Sisters, you can learn to control your emotions. So often you find it difficult to adjust your thinking away from feeling sorry for yourself. These may seem harsh words this morning, My Beloveds, but they are truth.

You enjoy an occasional down day. There is some satisfaction in an occasional taste of melancholy, but much of your sadness is a learned habit from your childhood, where you enjoyed the attention from your negative actions.

Take a little time today to consider the possibility that you may be using your negative thinking and speaking to draw attention to yourselves.

It may have become a technique that you use to gain attention, just as you did when you were a child."

See your self...taking the suggested few minutes to examine the possibility that "you" do use negativity "to gain attention." Great maturity is required now to leave all the childish attention gaining habits behind.

December 6
Mind Control

"You must learn to appreciate that negative emotions are counter-productive and that you can simply change your thoughts from negative to positive by a concentrated act of your will. I have told you this before. But you habituate your negative thinking.

Negative thinking *always* wastes our precious time. I will tell you this often. You need to be reminded so that you will set your thinking on the correction of this little habit that is simply a residual from a childish thought life.

I will have you look around you and discern how so many of your Brothers and Sisters use negative thinking to control one another. Once you recognize the habit as derogatory, you can learn to put it aside."

See your self...fully recognizing the counter-productivity of negative thinking. Do you really need it? You certainly do not need it if you consider how valuable your time is to you.

December 7
Love One Another Today

"Beloveds, there are many little habits left over from your childhood. But we will concentrate now on the simple fact that negative thinking is a waste of time. The days go quickly by and you often spend them thinking about situations that you can do little to change.

Can you change the past? Of course not! Yet think how much time you spend just going over again in your mind some action of yesterday or last week or last year. You cannot change the past and yet you often waste a precious new day by reliving what you cannot change. Why do you do this, My Brothers and Sisters?

Ah, the answer is simple. It is a habit. And habits are something that you can do something about. You can begin to put away thoughts about the irreparable past and begin to use today to its best advantage. Stay in the moment."

See your self...releasing the past completely. Live in the perfection of now, ever prepared to use every today to its best advantage.

December 8
Yesterday, Today And Forever

"Again I say to you that you must put the past away. Lay it aside as you would a garment that has long outworn its usefulness. Forget the past. You cannot change it. But you can do something constructive with today. Now, in the present, do your best to fulfill our Father's Love Commandment to love one another today.

I have also told you not to worry about the future. I want you to understand fully that your future is in Father's Hands. Be in My peace."

See your self...expecting somewhere in the gift of this beautiful day, to have the opportunity to fulfill our Father's Love commandment to love as He would have you love.

December 9
Stay In The Present

"It is time to work on staying in the present. And I tell you this truth. For a great majority of our Father's Children, learning to live in the present is indeed, a labor, a work that will require much concentration.

The past is gone and tomorrow has not yet come. Today is the focus of our concentration. You are to think about the hours ahead only as they happen, one day at a time, for you know that plans often go awry.

You awaken and the hours lay before you. You have daily chores to accomplish. There are things you may desire to do in the hours ahead. These hours can go your way as planned or something unavoidable may occur to change the path of the whole day. Learn to be flexible with the changes."

See your self...concentrating on gaining more flexibility. Change is inevitable and flexibility will greatly add to the peace we seek daily.

December 10
Expectations

"How many beautiful days in your lifetime have been spoiled because you could not accept the disappointment of a change in plans? You remember how often your emotions have spoiled the gift of a beautiful day. But you can learn to exchange your negative emotions. You can learn the simple acceptance to a change in plans.

Let the days unfold before you. Learn to set limited plans that allow for the unexpected. And then when the unexpected does develop, you will not be bothered with negative emotions. Expect the unexpected. You can be sure that it is inevitable."

*See your self...*mentally preparing for the inevitability of the unexpected. You are able to bypass the disappointment of emotional immaturity with just a measure of preparation.

December 11
Act In God's Time

"There is no hurry, My Beloveds; I have said this to you so many times before. You spend so much time rushing to and fro, trying to fill every moment with busyness. And you have filled all your days with plans that sometimes go awry.

Now I ask you to simply relax and let the days unfold. I AM not asking you to let go of the direction on your path. I AM simply asking you to stay in the moment. Release the past and let today unfold moment-by-moment. It will do that, unfold-by-moment, whether you plan it or not. Release all fear."

*See your self...*reminding your Self again today that the Father's Plan is perfect, and it is perfect "moment-by-moment." Releasing all fear becomes far easier in the light of His Plan's Perfection.

December 12
A Happy Attitude

"So much of your life could be so much happier if you simply learned to relax a little bit and let the days be as they happen. If I say today is a beautiful gift, could you simply believe that this is the truth and go into each moment in peace and gratitude?

Your attitude is a choice. Why not choose a happy attitude today? Why do I tell you this? Your attitude is connected to your thinking, and *every* thought, is a choice. If you don't like it, change it. Correct your thinking. Be of good cheer."

See your self...examining your attitude. Does it need an adjustment today? Then do it! Why be anything less than cheerful and happy? Why indeed! Do not forget Who takes your hand each day and walks the Path with you.

December 13
Emotional Maturity

"Do you enjoy the fearful days? Do you like to worry and fret? Of course, you do not! You can change anything you do not like. You can change any emotion that does not produce happiness.

We will work *together* to break many of these foolish habits learned in childhood. You will attain emotional maturity. Trust these words. Let the truth sink deeply into your thoughts now and bring a happy beginning to the beautiful gift of this day.

Yes, My Brothers and Sisters, a happy attitude is a choice."

See your self...growing daily in this promise for emotional maturity. Every foolish habit will be removed as you work *together* with the great I AM.

December 14
The Art Of Manipulation

"As children you learned the art of manipulation. You learned at a very young age this form of control. So many children rule the kingdom of their parents by their attitudes.

You know this is the truth. The children rule the roost. How has this happened? All by attitude!

Understand the principle. If you want something, you have learned that an unhappy attitude will get the attention of anyone who notices it. And you also have learned how to make your attitude noticed. This, too, is a habit learned in childhood.

You know that whatever attitude you choose controls both your mental and physical environment. So is it better to choose a happy attitude over any other? Of course it is! Choose to control your attitude."

See your self...learning to control your attitude; and by doing so you give up the childish attitude of controlling others. They must learn to control themselves.

December 15
Stop Complaining

"Change your thinking, My Brothers and Sisters, and you change your world. I would tell you today that so much of your thinking is a waste of precious time. You are all very talented, each in your own unique way. Yes, you are creative beings.

Yet, you busy your thought life with non-essentials. And over your lifetime you have all become creatures of much non-essential thinking. Recognize the habit as wasteful and get on to the attention of the important. Use the time and energy to get on to the actual calling of your creativity. Time is passing and you have valuable work to do."

See your self...recognizing fully that you are a unique and creative human being. And take the necessary steps each day to fulfill you unique creative appointment.

December 16
Our Father's Business

"What will we do with all the time you redeem by removing senseless time consuming habits? You will simply return your thinking to our Father's Business.

There is a Kingdom to establish. You are going to be instrumental in the establishment of our Father's Kingdom on earth. This is the enterprise that provides the greatest satisfaction.

Each of you should be delighted to take your appointed place within this Family Business. We will be busy together in the days ahead, as step-by-step we remove all the non-essentials that you habituate. It will lead to heaven on earth."

See your self...as one of our Father's most ambitious workers. You are actively employed in our Father's Family Business and you work daily to establish His loving Kingdom on earth.

December 17
Our Father's Desire

"It is not easy, My Brothers and Sisters, to lay aside the unpleasant attitudes and replace them with a choice for happiness. This will take effort. But the effort will bring amazing results.

You are still skeptical that you are in control of your emotions. For far too long you have believed that your emotions simply happened to you, that you were, indeed, the victim of your feelings.

Feelings come and go in an instant. And you can take control over *any* emotion. I have proved this to you on an earlier occasion. Now I wish to return your focus to the *practice* of happiness."

*See your self...*involved in an all out effort to practice happiness. Could it be that with practice, happiness would one day become your standard of excellence? Why not try to habituate happiness?

December 18
The Gift Of Quiet Joy

"Yes, My Beloveds, a happy attitude is your gift to all your Brothers and Sisters that share the Path with you today. And a happy attitude is infectious. It is an easy gift to pass on to others.

How easy it is to allow circumstances to quickly change your attitude. You can change from happiness to great gloom in an instant. And how often this happens. Then with a reversal of circumstance the attitude again changes.

Can you really change the circumstances with the attitude change? Yes! And is it possible to be happy when the circumstances are unpleasant? Yes, for we trust fully in our Father's Presence in *every* circumstance."

*See your self...*remembering in the chaos of life, the words from sacred scripture..."For He causes *all* things to work for the good of those who love Him... and then even the unpleasant can be endured in happiness.

December 19
Accept The Challenges

"My Brothers and Sisters, today, like any other day, may offer you a challenge or two. Expect the unexpected, for in truth, there will always be little surprises along the path and not always pleasant ones.

Be prepared to look at every challenge as an opportunity for growth;

perhaps as an educational experience, or as a soul-expanding, life-enhancing challenge along the path.

You do not grow in the pleasant places. These are little rests in your Path. You grow in the challenges. Learn to enjoy the rigor it requires to meet these tests and to master the lessons.

Every challenge has its place for you to ascend to a higher level in your maturation. Accept the challenges, every one of them, as necessary.

Do not fight the process. Fighting the process is counter-productive. Learn to accept them calmly, in peace, and as part of our Father's Will."

*See your self...*accepting calmly the challenges as necessary. No need to fight the process when you understand the Father's Will for your continual growth in every challenge.

December 20
Accept The Gift Of Life

"As you mature you will learn to simply greet the challenges as necessary. Your thinking process already accepts My daily guidance, and surely it is the necessary guidance that you need on the Path.

You are growing very quickly now in the understanding of our Father's Will on earth. He desires that you accept the gift of life, with all the challenges it presents, as His Will on Earth for each and every one of His much-loved Children. Yes, you, indeed, are all loved beyond measure."

*See your self...*as an immeasurably loved child and accepting all the challenges that this precious gift of life presents.

December 21
Challenges Are Necessary

"Challenges are necessary, My Beloveds. You will learn to accept them as a necessary part of your growth process. And in truth, challenges keep the life process very exciting, do they not?

Yes, you may not like some of the challenges. You may resent the unpleasant ones, but acceptance is the easy course of action. You cannot change the process. You can change your attitude though, in every challenge.

Life can present great difficulties and you already have experienced many of life's difficult challenges. Now think of your attitude in the difficulties. For the most part you greet difficult challenges with anger or disappointment. I can show you the better Path."

See your self..giving up resentment, anger and disappointment in life's challenges. You are eager and very willing to accept the better Path.

December 22
A Happy Life

"In the setting of any goal, you know you need to take certain steps to reach that goal. A happy life is a worthy goal. And happiness, constant happiness takes concentrated effort.

It has been said that happiness is a choice. This is a great truth. Our Father's Desire is for His Children's happiness. Knowing this truth should set your Path straightaway towards the fruition of His Desire.

Those who seek our Father's Will on earth seek happiness both for themselves and for all their Brothers and Sisters. It is a worthy goal and it is our daily goal *together.*"

*See your self...*embracing this truth that our Father's Desire is for your happiness. This very thought in your day should bring you great delight.

December 23
Kingdom Principles

"Yes, there are obstacles to our goal, but none that cannot be met and removed. Our daily task is to embrace wholeheartedly our Father's Business. Step by step and hand in hand we go.

Welcome the gift of today and do all you can to bring yourself into alignment with the principles of the Kingdom. You will learn to follow the Path in peace and love and joy. You will learn all the secrets of a happy, peaceful life on earth full of good will towards all mankind."

*See your self...*knowing you *will* learn all the secrets of a happy, peace-filled life; and patiently desiring that happy, peace-filled life for all your Brothers and Sisters.

December 24
You Are All Precious Gifts

"You know that babies are precious gifts. Yes, all babies are gifts to life, each born as a blessing to all creation. Each of you has been born into this life as a gift to life.

Did you notice the words "each of you," My Brothers and Sisters? You have talents unrealized. You have the gift of love to give to all you meet.

And I will tell you today that it is My pleasure to teach you how to develop your gift, the gift of *you*.

Love one another. I have said this to you often, and you will hear Me say these words many times in the course of our time together. Your Love is His Gift."

*See your self...*as the gift our Father has prepared to carry His Love forward into this day and all the days ahead.

December 25
The Gift Of Brotherhood

"It is our Father's Desire that each of your realize what a gift you are and what great gifts you each are to each other. Take a moment to think of all the wonderful Brothers and Sisters that you know. And you have only just begun to realize the immensity of the Family that you have been born into.

The brotherhood of humankind *is* the Family of God in its entirety. You *will* grow in the knowledge of this Family. You will begin to understand the Love of God when you fully consider your true relationship one to another, and each of you to Him. He *is* Our Father."

*See your self...*accepting your personal membership in His Family. It *is* the Brotherhood of Love and you *will* advance mightily as one of His most willing Ambassadors.

December 26
A Loving Response

"There is a loving response in every situation. You know the loving ways of the kingdom of heaven within. You know how to choose the better Path. Now let us be about our Father's Business today.

Do not forget to smile often. The insignia of love will always lighten the path for some Brother or Sister. Use it often. It will always bring happy, loving results. Take the time to smile before you speak. Choose to convey only loving responses in all your conversations.

Taking a few extra minutes to choose the proper response to the negative situations will always produce positive results. You can always make a better choice in your words and actions with a slight hesitancy before you act."

*See your self...*learning the very positive habit of simply thinking before you speak.

December 27
You Grow Daily

"Indeed, My Beloveds, you are leaning the lessons of Kingdom Living. Step by step we do walk this Path together in the earth experience.

You have put away many of the attitudes from your childhood. As the lessons are revealed, you are putting aside the attitudes representative of self-will and more and more with greater frequency you are putting on the happy attitudes of His Will, as the Children of our Father's glorious Image.

Father knows of your struggles each day to walk the Path in the Light of His Will. Yet each day the Path grows easier to walk. Your rarely stumble into the ways of your childhood learning. You grow daily in the life Father Wills for each of you. And in this We are most pleased."

*See your self...*more aware of your continuing journey in the Kingdom principles. And yes, recognizing that the Path is growing easier as you consistently advance.

December 28
Light On The Path

"A new day begins. In a sense it is the same as many days before and many days ahead. Smiles and happy attitudes cast the Light of His Love, shining through you, on the Pathway before us. Yes, the Pathway will always be illuminated by the generosity of your happy attitudes.

There is no doubt now in your mind that self-will has no place in the Illumined Life. Go forward and greet this day in happiness. You desire no other will but Father's. And His Business of loving one another is the only business that you need care about today."

*See your self...*using smiles and a happy attitude to shine our Father's illuminating Love-light to all the Brothers and Sisters that you meet on the Path today. Let His Business consistently be your business.

December 29
Delight In Lessons Learned

"Yes, My Brothers and Sisters, I come to you all each day as the Teacher of our Father's Will on earth.

He delights in each lesson accomplished by each and every one of His most Beloved Children. Your happiness is easily obtained in the attitudes of kingdom living. Love, joy, peace and continual happiness are the rewards obtained by those who practice the Laws of our Father's universal Will.

You have learned that your daily forgiveness account is to be kept with great conscientiousness. Gentleness and kindness are the bywords of those who walk in our Father's Image."

*See your self...*walking the Path in love, joy, peace and happiness. It is not a dream but reality for those who practice daily our Father's Will.

December 30
Let Your Light Shine

"As we near the close of this incredible year of learning and teaching in Father's Curriculum, let Me pause to observe the Light that shines within you and to rejoice in it.

You desire only Love, and in that desire you have elected to remain constant as His Lovers of Humankind. Be strong today in this curriculum of Love. Let the grace and great beauty of your chosen Path illumine the Path for all those whom you encounter today.

You are learning that peace belongs to all those who are meek in spirit. A gentle reminder now and then is all you need to keep you walking in the great Light of our Father's Will. There is no turning back.

The Light *is* spreading, My Brothers and Sisters. And yes, you will illumine the Path for many by your chosen consistency to the details of Kingdom Living. Yes, each of you are a beacon of His Light. Let your little light shine."

> *See your self*...aglow with His Light! You *are* His chosen Ones! You are His ever glowing Lamp Lighters and that is a very great truth.

December 31
Happy New Year

"Beloveds, it has been an interesting year, has it not? Yes, of course, it has been. There have been many days of mysteries solved and challenges met. The tasks that have been accomplished assure us that no task will be beyond our endurance for its fulfillment.

You and I have come far on the Path, but in truth we have far to go and much to accomplish in the year ahead.

But fear not! The New Year beacons now with much to delight us. Step happily forward, for we wear the uniforms and the insignias of Love. We have mastered the simple rules of our Father's Service. Now all that remains in the tasks ahead is our diligence to the doing of His Will.

And I AM with you!"

> *See your self*...forever hand-in-hand with our Master Teacher and Friend. Is there any thing beyond the capability of this perfect combination of exquisite Love and Friendship? Absolutely not!

Printed in the United States
By Bookmasters